March 25, 2005

To Chris,

With my love always.

Grandma

Tuskegee Airmen
American Heroes

Tuskegee Airmen
AMERICAN HEROES

By Lynn M. Homan and
Thomas Reilly

Illustrated by
Rosalie M. Shepherd

PELICAN PUBLISHING COMPANY
Gretna 2002

*The word "Pelican" and the depiction of a pelican are trademarks
of Pelican Publishing Company, Inc., and are registered
in the U.S. Patent and Trademark Office.*

Library of Congress Cataloging-in-Publication Data

Homan, Lynn M.
  Tuskegee airmen : American heroes / by Lynn M. Homan and
Thomas Reilly ; illustrated by Rosalie M. Shepherd.
      p. cm.
Includes bibliographical references.
  ISBN 1-56554-994-5 (alk. paper)
  1. World War, 1939-1945—Aerial operations, American—Juvenile
literature. 2. African American air pilots—History—Juvenile litera-
ture. 3. Tuskegee Army Air Field (Ala.)—Juvenile literature. 4.
World War, 1939-1945—Participation, African American—Juvenile
literature. I. Reilly, Thomas. II. Shepherd, Rosalie M. III. Title.
  D790 .H658 2002
  940.54'4973—dc21
                                        2002007054

Printed in the United States of America
Published by Pelican Publishing Company, Inc.
1000 Burmaster Street, Gretna, Louisiana 70053

To the memory of our friend, Louis Purnell, and to all of the other men and women who participated in the Tuskegee Experience. Although Victor Kennedy and his students are imaginary, the story of the Tuskegee Airmen is true.

—L. M. H. and T. R.

Contents

Preface

When we fly on an airplane today, it's not unusual for the pilot to greet us at the door and welcome us on board. It's also not unusual for the pilot to be an African-American. A few years ago, that wouldn't have been possible. Black men and women were not hired as airline pilots. There also weren't any black pilots in the Air Force, army, navy, or Marine Corps. That may seem unbelievable today, but it was definitely the case in 1941 when America entered World War II. America was fighting against the Axis powers—Germany, Italy, and Japan—and there weren't enough pilots to fly fighters, bombers, and transport airplanes. In spite of that, African-American men were not allowed to serve their country as pilots in the Air Force, or, as it was called then, the Army Air Corps, just because they were black.

The Wright brothers flew the world's first airplane at Kitty Hawk, North Carolina, in 1903. Black men and women began flying airplanes only a few years later. It wasn't easy. Most white instructors would not accept African-Americans as flight students. They usually wouldn't teach women to fly either. It was also very hard to find someone willing to sell an airplane to an African-American or do mechanical work on the plane. In spite of all the difficulties, however, young black men and women didn't give up.

Often African-Americans went to France to learn to fly airplanes because the racial climate there was more accepting. In fact, two of America's best-known, pioneer, African-American aviators did just that. Eugene Jacques Bullard learned to fly in France and then, during World War I, became a pilot for the Lafayette Flying Corps. A young black woman named Bessie Coleman convinced two Frenchmen, Gaston and René Caudron, to teach her to fly. In June 1921, she became the first African-American to hold a pilot's license.

When World War II broke out in Europe in 1939, hundreds of African-Americans already knew how to fly airplanes. Over and over again, they applied to the Army Air Corps to be pilots, but the U.S. government always refused to accept them. There was no place for African-American pilots in the Army Air Corps. America was a seg-regated country, and only white men could be military pilots.

All of that would eventually change. Why? Much of the credit belongs to a group known today as the Tuskegee Airmen. Who are the Tuskegee Airmen? Ask the person working the counter at your favorite fast-food restaurant. Ask your mothers, fathers, or grandpar-ents. Ask someone sitting next to you in school or church. Chances are, no one will know. Who are the Tuskegee Airmen? This is their story.

Tuskegee Airmen
American Heroes

Chapter One

The Lesson Begins

It was the middle of the school year at Martin Luther King, Jr., Middle School in Washington, D.C. The weather had been especially bad. Every night Sunny Skye, the forecaster on the television news, told viewers that this had been one of the worst winters since the U.S. National Weather Service had been keeping records, which was more than one hundred years earlier. Tonight, she had good news. The cold and snowy winter was about to break—at least temporarily. She was predicting warm, sunny weather for the next few days.

While that was welcome news to most of the population of Washington, D.C., it was not exactly what Sharon Riggs, the principal of Martin Luther King, Jr., Middle School, wanted to hear. The unseasonably warm temperatures would result in a flood of absences; students would stay home in droves. She didn't like that, but there was really nothing she could do about it as long as they returned with notes from their parents or guardians. Unfortunately for the principal, teachers would also be absent, and that was a problem she would have to handle. Substitute teachers would have to be found, and the great weather forecast would make getting them difficult. Like everyone else, they would want to enjoy the first warm weather of the year.

Twenty-five phone calls later, she had several substitute teachers lined up. She was still one short. She knew that she'd need someone to cover Mr. McCormack's American-history classes. She was certain that he would be a no-show. He always was when the weather got warm. A quick phone call to her assistant, Marge Kennedy, seemed to offer the solution to the problem.

"Sharon, my father would be glad to cover the schedule for you."

"I appreciate that, Marge, but I don't know if it's such a good idea. He's never taught before, has he? And he is quite a bit older than most of our other substitutes. Kids always try to take advantage of subs anyway."

"Sharon, he can do it. He's never taught middle school before, but he's been an educator all of his life. As for McCormack's classes, don't worry, the kids will love him."

"Marge, I really do need another substitute for tomorrow—probably even for the rest of the week. But if the kids drive him out screaming, don't say I didn't warn you."

Sunny Skye's weather forecast from the night before was right on target. By 7 A.M. Wednesday morning, teachers had already started calling in sick. It was going to be a textbook case of the schoolhouse flu, brought on by the first warm weather of the year. By 7:30, hundreds of seventh, eighth, and ninth graders streamed through the wide doors of Martin Luther King, Jr., Middle School. Backpacks weighed them down as they headed toward their homerooms.

Victor Kennedy stood in front of Room 12 and watched with great interest as thirty teenagers stood in the hall, appearing to be in no particular hurry for Mr. McCormack's first-period American-history class. They already knew that McCormack was not coming and that the old man at the door was going to be their substitute teacher. For the most part, they simply ignored him.

Concerned that her worst fears were becoming a reality, Sharon Riggs decided that she had better make sure the situation didn't get totally out of hand. She didn't want to hurt the old man's feelings, but she couldn't have thirty seventh-grade students roaming the halls for the next hour.

"All right class, let's go. I want everyone in the room, now." Slowly, the class began its movement toward the open door. Once they started, the group took on the appearance of a long multicolored centipede, their arms and legs moving in the same direction.

"Do we have to, Mrs. Riggs? What's this old geezer gonna teach us?" These were good kids, and she knew they meant no disrespect to Mr. Kennedy, but she feared that he would take the comments to heart and be insulted.

"I want you all in your seats right now. You will sit there, you will be quiet, and you will show Mr. Kennedy some respect. Is that understood?"

"Yes, Mrs. Riggs," they halfheartedly muttered.

Victor Kennedy walked to the front of the room, nodded, and mouthed, "I've got it now, thanks." The principal headed for the door, giving the class one last look of warning. She had a school to run. The old man would just have to fend for himself. Nonetheless, she felt as if she was leaving him in a lion cage without the whip and chair for protection. The kids were going to eat him alive.

Mr. Kennedy stood in front of the class for several seconds, saying nothing as he observed the group. Sensing his hesitation, the gentle rumbling of voices quickly became a blend of noises as books dropped, desks scraped across the floor, and thirty teenagers began to talk in unison. The depth of his voice surprised them as they suddenly heard the old man introduce himself.

"My name is Victor Kennedy."

"Ooh," he heard from the back of the room, but other than that, the class became quiet as the students looked in his direction. Picking up a piece of chalk, Kennedy scrawled one word on the blackboard.

"Does anyone know what this means?" Blank stares and negative head-shakes met his question. "Can anyone pronounce this word?" A couple of quiet, tentative attempts resulted. "Tuskegee," said Kennedy, "is a small town in Alabama."

"What's that got to do with us?" he heard from several of the seventh graders.

"Tuskegee, Alabama, was the site of Tuskegee Institute, one of America's first African-American colleges."

"Big deal," came the response.

"Yes, class, it is a big deal. It wasn't that many years ago that America was a segregated country."

"What's that supposed to mean?" several boys and girls spoke at the same time.

"It means that Americans were separated by race in almost every aspect of daily life. Blacks and whites lived apart from each other. They went to different schools and churches, ate at different restaurants, attended separate movie theaters, and even shopped at different stores. Everything was separate."

"No way," said a girl named Tiffany.

"Oh yes," Kennedy said. "Black people were not allowed to go to places where white people went. And what's more, segregation was not just a custom. In many places, especially in the South, it was also the law."

"Nope, that's not true," said a voice from the front row.

"Unfortunately, it's true. African-Americans had to use separate rest rooms and couldn't drink out of the same water fountains used by white people. If they rode the bus, they had to sit in the back. Or if they took a trip on the train, they were forced to sit in a separate car called the Jim Crow car."

"That's not fair," said Makayla, a tall black girl with braces on her teeth.

"No, it wasn't fair, it wasn't right, and it was very cruel. But for many years, it's the way things were," said Kennedy.

"But I still don't know what that has to do with us," argued Luis, a Hispanic boy seated in the back of the room.

"Look around this class." Thirty faces turned right and left. "What do you see?" Victor Kennedy asked. No one answered. Kennedy repeated the question. "What do you see?" This time, a young white girl named Charlene very slightly raised her hand, and Kennedy nodded in her direction.

"Kids," she said.

"That's right, kids. But tell me more."

"Just kids," Charlene repeated.

"But where are you all from?" asked Kennedy.

"All over," said an African-American student named Marcus.

"That's right, all over. Look around again. You're from all over. There are white faces, black faces, Hispanic faces, and even some

Asian ones. Not so many years ago, you couldn't have been in this school together. That's what this has to do with all of you."

Just then, Mrs. Riggs looked into the classroom, expecting turmoil. Instead, the room was quiet. Kennedy had their attention. Victor Kennedy noticed Mrs. Riggs at the door and gave her just a hint of a smile. She nodded and returned to her office.

"Back in the 1940s, in the old days, long before any of you, your parents, or even some of your grandparents were born, there was a horrible war going on that effected the entire world. Have you studied World War II yet?"

"Yes sir," was the answer.

"Did your teacher tell you about the Tuskegee Airmen?" The answer was a collection of blank stares, "nopes," and thirty heads shaking left and right.

"Back before the United States entered World War II on December 7, 1941, it was becoming obvious that America would eventually be drawn into the war. Men and women began enlisting in the various branches of the service, and President Franklin Roosevelt and the military began getting ready for war, just in case. Do you remember what I told you earlier about America being a segregated country?"

They all nodded.

"Black people as well as white people were, of course, feeling patriotic, and they wanted to do their part to defend America. Even though the treatment African-Americans received was pretty horrible, it was still their country, and in time of war, they wanted to serve in the same ways as everyone else."

"And did they?" asked Charlene.

"Yes, but the options for African-Americans during World War II were pretty limited. Because of segregation, black men and women were not allowed to serve with whites. They had to be in separate units, and almost without exception, they were forced to do the most menial tasks."

"Like what?"

"Good question, Makayla. African-Americans were allowed to only do jobs such as digging ditches, cleaning the bases, and working in the kitchens: the worst jobs. Most blacks were in the army.

There were very few in either the navy or in the Army Air Corps. By the way, what was then known as the U.S. Army Air Corps is today's Air Force."

"Why did African-Americans stand for that? Why didn't they do something about it, Mr. Kennedy?" Marcus demanded.

"Well, they did. But they had to do it in their own way. Don't forget, America was a segregated country, and it was the law."

"I wouldn't take that from nobody," challenged Jamal.

"What would you do if someone treated you that way?" asked the substitute teacher.

Taking no time at all to think about his answer, the young man stood up. "I don't know. But I know I wouldn't put up with that from nobody, nohow. I'd get in their face; I'd straighten them out fast. I wouldn't let them treat me like that."

"Hmmm," said Kennedy. "Have you ever heard of lynching?"

A hand went up in the back of the room. "You mean, like a long time ago in the Old West, when the sheriff hung the bad guys?"

"Not exactly," Kennedy responded. "I'm talking about more recent times. Something that, unfortunately, was still a part of life in America. Sometimes, when people decided that a black person had committed some offense or even had just become too pushy, they would take matters into their own hands and, without any legal action, dispense what they considered to be appropriate punishment."

"What kind of punishment? What'd they do?"

"A mob, frequently made up of members of the Ku Klux Klan, dressed in white sheets and wearing hoods to hide their identity, would get a rope and hang the black person."

"That's not true," murmured the class almost in unison. "That couldn't happen here. Could it?"

"Class, I'm very sorry to tell you that it not only could happen, but did happen. And this went on for many years. America, especially in the South, was a very dangerous place for black Americans. So that's what it was like in America for black people at the time of World War II. The country was segregated; black people were forced to endure horrible Jim Crow laws meant to keep them in their place. But in spite of all of this, even though America was less than perfect, African-Americans wanted to help their country in time of war."

"But what does that have to do with Tuskegee, Mr. Kennedy?"

"That's a very good question, Luis, and I'm glad you asked it. I told you earlier that African-Americans couldn't serve in the Army Air Corps, except in small numbers and always in the least desirable jobs. What image do you have when you think of the Air Force?"

"That's easy," they shouted out, "airplanes!"

"Well," asked Kennedy, "what do you need to fly those airplanes?"

"Ah, Mr. Kennedy," they responded as if he had asked them a question far beneath their intelligence. "Duh, you have to have pilots to fly the airplanes." Kennedy laughed and nodded his head.

"Of course, you have to have pilots. And that's where Tuskegee, Alabama, comes into our story. For a lot of reasons, the War Department finally decided in 1941 that they would allow black men to be trained to fly airplanes as military pilots. This great experiment would unfold at a separate military base, Tuskegee Army Air Field. Except for the white personnel in charge of the base, Tuskegee Army Air Field would be reserved for African-Americans."

"That seems unfair and stupid," groaned most of the teenagers, black and white alike.

"Of course it was," said Kennedy. "It was stupid, unfair, and wrong, not to mention extremely expensive. But remember what I've said. The country was . . ."

"Segregated," roared thirty voices all at once.

"That's right," Kennedy said. "The country was segregated, but finally, the military had agreed to allow black men to fly military airplanes. According to the plan, at first there would be one squadron of black pilots. It would be made up of about thirty-five pilots and a couple hundred men who would be needed to support them. The squadron would be called the 99th Pursuit Squadron, although eventually its name would be changed to the 99th Fighter Squadron."

"Why did they need so many other people?" questioned Charlene.

"Well, there were all kinds of things that had to be done. They needed people to fix the airplanes, cook meals, process paperwork, and do lots of other jobs. It took anywhere from ten to fifteen people to keep one pilot flying. And that was just for the 99th Fighter Squadron. As far as running a big military base such as Tuskegee was concerned, there had to be support personnel there, too—both men and women, military and civilian, black and white.

"In June 1941, thirteen African-American men reported to Tuskegee Institute for pilot training. The first class of black flight cadets included Captain Benjamin O. Davis, Jr.; John C. Anderson, Jr.; Charles Brown; Theodore Brown; Marion Carter; Lemuel R. Custis; Charles DeBow; Frederick H. Moore; Ulysses S. Pannell; George S. Roberts; William Slade; Mac Ross; and Roderick Williams."

Pham, one of the Asian students in the class, raised his hand with a question. "Mr. Kennedy, didn't you say that they were going to be trained at Tuskegee Army Air Field?"

"Yes, I did, and eventually the training would be at the military airfield. But it wasn't completed yet. It was still under construction."

"Mr. Kennedy, why would the government set up a training base in a place like Tuskegee, Alabama? If the South was as segregated as you said, that seems like the worst possible place for a base for African-Americans. Why not in a place like Chicago or New York?"

"There were a lot of reasons, Pham. Certainly, one of the main reasons was because of Tuskegee Institute. With the exception of, perhaps, Howard University right here in Washington, D.C., Tuskegee Institute was the best known of all of the black colleges in the United States. The president of Tuskegee Institute, Frederick Patterson, very much wanted the black pilot-training program at Tuskegee, and he worked very hard to get the government to put it in Alabama. There were other reasons as well, and one of the most important was a man named C. Alfred Anderson. Nicknamed 'Chief,' Anderson was in charge of the early flight training at Tuskegee Institute. He had an excellent reputation, and the Air Corps really had a lot of respect for him. And let's not forget the weather factor. What happens in the Northern or Midwestern states in the winter?"

A sea of hands went up. When Kennedy pointed to the middle of the class, the response was "snow."

"That's right. There's snow, it's cold, and sometimes it's not good flying weather. So from that standpoint, it made great sense to build Tuskegee Army Air Field in Alabama. But there was another reason. The military really didn't want the training program to succeed. They didn't want black men flying airplanes, and they wanted the program to fail. They knew the racial attitudes of many people in Alabama would make it that much harder for the African-Americans to succeed." That statement drew hoots and hollers and cries of disbelief. "I know, class. It's hard to believe that the military would establish a training program that they wanted to fail—especially in time of war. But that's exactly what they did."

"Why would they do that?" the class exclaimed almost as one.

"It all comes down to one thing. The men in charge of both the government and the Army Air Corps did not want black men to fly military airplanes. What they really wanted was for this program to fail and fail miserably so that they could use the outcome as proof that African-Americans simply did not have the intelligence to be pilots."

"That's just stupid," threw out one kid after another.

"Yes," said Kennedy. "It was stupid, but back then, the Army Air Corps would do almost anything to prove that black men were not qualified to be pilots. Remember, as I've told you several times, America was segregated. There were no African-American pilots in the Air Corps, and many people wanted to keep it that way."

"But, Mr. Kennedy, they proved them wrong, didn't they? They did learn how to fly, didn't they?"

"Yes, they did, Makayla. They sure did. Let me tell you how."

Chapter Two

The 99th Fighter Squadron

"While construction workers built Tuskegee Army Air Field, the first flight cadets began fifteen weeks of primary training on the campus of Tuskegee Institute. Classes included ground school, weather conditions, and the principles of flight. On July 19, 1941, Major General Walter R. Weaver, the commander of the Southeast Training Center, encouraged the thirteen men who hoped to be the first African-American Air Corps pilots: 'The eyes of your country and the eyes of your people are upon you.' At the same time, he warned them, 'You cannot be inoculated with the ability to fly. The life of a flying student is no bed of roses.'"

"Mr. Kennedy, didn't you say something about the men on the ground?" asked Luis. "You know, like the mechanics? What about them?"

"That's right, I did. While the pilots were training at Tuskegee, other African-Americans were being trained as ground and support crews at Chanute Field, not far from Rantoul, Illinois. They didn't join up with the pilots at Tuskegee for several months. By then, the flight cadets had finished primary training and were ready for the secondary phase at Tuskegee Army Air Field."

"Who trained the pilots at Tuskegee? Were the trainers other Air Corps pilots?"

"That's a very interesting question, Jamal, and the answer may surprise you. The training program consisted of four phases—preflight, primary, basic, and advanced. During the later portions, the flight instructors were military men, but during the first part, the instructors were civilians. A very important thing to remember is that most of those civilian flight instructors were black. Many of them also wanted to serve as military pilots, but they were just too valuable as instructors there at Tuskegee."

"Mr. Kennedy, did the whites and blacks at Tuskegee get along okay?"

"That's hard to answer, Pham. Certainly, in the town of Tuskegee, things were pretty bad. The whites that lived in Tuskegee didn't want flight training for African-Americans to take place near their town. There were frequent complaints about how the black men behaved; the white residents drafted petitions and filed protests about the activities of Tuskegee Army Air Field. Tuskegee, Alabama, could be a very dangerous place for young black men. Many of the African-Americans stationed at Tuskegee Army Air Field chose never to go into town for just that reason.

"But I think that conditions on the campus and on the base were different. The black flight instructors at Tuskegee, and many of the white instructors as well, wanted the flight cadets to succeed, and they worked very hard to give the best flight training possible. Captain Davis was first in the class to solo. The others would soon have their own opportunity to hear their flight instructor tell them to 'take it up on your own and make sure you get back down alive.' The training was quite intense, and unfortunately, everyone didn't make it through the program. Before the end of training, eight of the first thirteen cadets had been eliminated from the program."

"That must have been horrible for them," Charlene said. Several other students nodded in agreement.

"You're right, it was. Those eight men had given everything they had to the program, but it just wasn't enough. I guess they just weren't cut out to be military pilots."

"Mr. Kennedy, what happened to them after that?" asked Luis with a worried expression on his face.

"Well, there really wasn't any place else for them to go. They ended up as enlisted men, being trained to do something else. Their dream of becoming an officer and a fighter pilot was over."

"Was the training that hard?"

"Yes, it was, Tiffany. When the men first started out in the flying program, their training was dual. Flying with an instructor pilot, they learned the basics of flying an airplane. I know that this sounds easy, but many of the men had never even been in an airplane before. After about eight hours of instruction, the cadets were expected to make their solo flight.

"The cadets woke up every morning at 6 A.M. to the sound of a bugle playing reveille. All day long, they had physical training, ground school, and flight training, and at night, they studied. Eventually, in advanced training, they would learn night flying, and how to do things like loops and rolls, and combat flying. It wasn't easy. As the first class continued to train, more groups of men reported to Tuskegee."

"Gosh, Mr. Kennedy, that place must've been getting really crowded."

"You're right, Jamal. It was, and there was a great deal of tension. Life at Tuskegee was pretty primitive. Before the base was finished, men lived in the college dormitories. When there were too many people for that, tents were set up as living quarters. Imagine what it was like to live in a tent in the summer heat and rain of Alabama.

"By the fall of 1941, black men and women from all over the United States filled Tuskegee Army Air Field. Several hundred support personnel arrived from Chanute Field. The base became a self-sufficient city in the middle of the hostility and Jim Crow laws embraced by many of the white citizens of Tuskegee.

"One after another, additional classes of flying cadets entered the program at Tuskegee. Every single man had high hopes of having silver Air Corps wings pinned on his chest after graduating from the pilot-training program. For many of those who 'washed out' or were eliminated, that failure was something that they carried with them forever. You see, the possibility of failing was always part of training. Flight cadets could be, and often were, eliminated from the program at will. Each day, the cadets marched to the flight line and received their instructions. After flying, they might or might not receive an evaluation. Instructors handed out pink slips for flying infractions. If a cadet received three pink slips, he was gone from flight training."

"Mr. Kennedy, you told us that many of the men never left the base. What did they do?"

"That's another good question, Makayla. These men in the pilot-training program were obviously very dedicated. But even the most dedicated cadets needed some relaxation. I told you that there was an unwelcome atmosphere and a very strict policy of segregation that made visits into the town of Tuskegee not very pleasant. So most of the social and recreational activities had to be on the base.

"Physical fitness obviously was part of the army's formal training, but it was also part of the recreation program. Athletics were definitely part of the life at Tuskegee Army Air Field. There were swim meets, shooting competitions, and track-and-field events. There were baseball and football teams. The men were encouraged to take part in all of these activities."

"What about girls? Were there any girls there?" called out Marcus, who was immediately cheered on by his friends.

"Of course there were girls. Both men and women attended Tuskegee Institute. From time to time, there were dances at the base, and young women from nearby schools were always invited. One of the base commanders, Colonel Noel Parrish, strongly believed in the well-being of the men and women on the base, and he did everything that he could to make life a little more pleasant."

"What kinds of things? What'd he do?" asked Jamal.

"Well, it's important to keep in mind that Colonel Parrish was actually the third commander at the airfield. The first commander, Major James Ellison, seemed to care about the welfare of the men, but he quickly got into trouble with the local residents when he openly showed his support for the black fliers. This led to his removal as commanding officer of Tuskegee Army Air Field."

"That doesn't seem fair," Jamal protested.

"Maybe not. But worse than being unfair for Major Ellison, it was not good for the morale and well-being of those assigned to Tuskegee Army Air Field."

"Why was that?"

"Because the next commander, Colonel Frederick von Kimble, did not believe in the same things in which Major Ellison had believed."

"Like what?" asked Luis.

"Well, for starters, von Kimble believed that one of his most important duties was to keep the leaders of the town of Tuskegee happy, even if it was to the detriment of the men and women on the base. For another thing, Colonel von Kimble believed in segregation. Even if blacks and whites had done things together previously, von Kimble now discouraged it. As part of his policy of segregation, von Kimble ordered that many of the facilities on the base be segregated and marked with Colored or White signs. His message was clear. Like it or not, African-Americans stationed at Tuskegee Army Air Field had no choice but to obey the signs."

"No way!" the class jeered as one.

"Fortunately for the success of the future of Tuskegee Army Air Field, Colonel von Kimble was eventually promoted and reassigned to another base."

"Yea," rang out a chorus of youthful voices. A smile flashed on Kennedy's lined face.

"One of the first things that Colonel Parrish did after he took over as Tuskegee Army Air Field's commanding officer was to have those awful Colored and White signs taken down. And he did what he could to integrate the base as much as possible. You know, he urged whites and blacks on the base to do things together, believing that it encouraged friendships among the men.

"Another thing that Colonel Parrish did was bring in celebrities to entertain the troops at Tuskegee Army Air Field. He arranged appearances by Cab Calloway, Ella Fitzgerald, Lena Horne, and heavyweight boxer Joe Louis to help boost morale at the base."

Tiffany spoke up, "Mr. Kennedy, we've never heard of any of those people."

"That's too bad, since they were all very famous black entertainers of the era.

"As I told you earlier, while the original group of men in the first class trained, additional hopeful pilots were assigned to Tuskegee.

It's hard to imagine, but in no time, the first class had completed their training and was ready for graduation.

"Captain Benjamin O. Davis, Jr.; Lemuel R. Custis; Charles DeBow; Mac Ross; and George S. Roberts sat in the audience on March 7, 1942, and listened to Major General George Stratemeyer: 'The vast unseen audience of your well-wishers senses that this graduation is an historic moment. . . . Future graduates of this school will look up to you as old pilots. They will be influenced profoundly by the examples you set.' When Stratemeyer ended his speech, the five men finally realized their dream as the base commander pinned silver Air Corps wings to their uniforms. The celebration was dimmed only by the fact that, of the thirteen men who had started in the program, only five had graduated."

Pham had another question. "Mr. Kennedy, did they go to war after graduation?"

"Not for quite a while. There were only five trained pilots. And it would be quite some time before there were enough pilots and crews to make up an entire squadron that was ready for combat."

"Well, Mr. Kennedy, why didn't they just transfer them to another squadron so that they could help win the war right away?"

"Well, Pham, I guess the biggest reason was segregation. Even though there was a war going on in Europe, the United States military just wasn't ready yet for black men to be part of a white squadron."

"When did they finally go to Europe?" Jamal wanted to know.

"Well, it was almost a year later. But before we get to that part of the story, let's talk a little about what was still going on here at home. Do you remember that I told you it took ten to fifteen people on the ground to support each pilot? Can you think of what kinds of jobs those people might have been doing?"

"Fixing the airplanes?" suggested one of the students.

"Building the buildings and the runways, stuff like that," offered Marcus.

"That's right, and those were certainly important. You may not have even thought about some other kinds of jobs, not to mention the people who did them. For example, although they weren't allowed to serve in combat overseas, women held lots of jobs at Tuskegee."

"You mean as secretaries and stuff?" Charlene asked.

"Well, that's one of the jobs. A base the size of Tuskegee required lots of administrative personnel, and many of them were women."

"I know, Mr. Kennedy. They were nurses."

"That's true, Tiffany. Some of the women were nurses. In fact, Tuskegee's chief nurse, Della Raney, was the first African-American nurse to report for duty during World War II. But women also held some pretty unusual jobs. For example, what do you need to have when you jump out of an airplane?"

"That's easy, Mr. Kennedy. Everybody knows you need a parachute," Luis answered.

"You're exactly right. For that parachute to open correctly, however, it has to be packed in a certain way. The person in charge of the Parachute Department at Tuskegee Army Air Field was Alice Dungy Gray. Before the war started, she had been a schoolteacher in Louisiana. Her assistant was also a woman.

"Mrs. Lillie Drew was the dietician in charge of planning the thousands of meals served each day at Tuskegee. Carrie Campbell worked as a guard at the base. Mrs. Young ran the control tower. Just as the men did, women held all kinds of jobs.

"By the middle of 1942, there were more than three thousand people assigned to Tuskegee Army Air Field. The base was bursting at the seams, as almost every month more cadets graduated. Now fully manned with pilots and support personnel, the 99th Fighter Squadron was ready to go. At the same time, additional squadrons were being formed."

"Mr. Kennedy, since there were now lots of trained pilots, why didn't they join the war?" Pham asked again.

"Well, they wanted to. They had been waiting for this for so long, and they were certainly well trained, but there was still one very big problem, Pham."

"What was that?"

"The Army Air Corps simply didn't know what to do with them or where to send them. So as the African-American squadrons prepared to spend yet another year, 1943, training at Tuskegee, the men of the 99th sat and waited for orders to ship out."

"What'd they do all that time, Mr. Kennedy?"

"They trained, trained, and trained some more, Charlene. Benjamin O. Davis, Jr., who had by this time been promoted to lieutenant colonel, made his feelings quite clear when he told his men, 'My greatest desire is to lead this squadron to victory against the enemy.'"

"Mr. Kennedy, these men must really have been very brave and very patient to put up with this for so long." Makayla expressed the opinion of most of the class.

"Indeed, they were. When we talk about life at Tuskegee, we need always to keep in mind what life was like for black men and women in America at the time. We've already talked about segregation at length, but I'm not sure that I really made it clear just how bad it was. Life really was a struggle for African-Americans. In many places, they couldn't vote, get a quality education, or even a decent job."

"Was it that bad all over the country?" questioned Luis.

"Has anyone heard of the Mason-Dixon line?" A couple of hands went up and Kennedy called on Jamal.

"I think it was kind of like the border between Northern and Southern states, wasn't it?"

"Yes, it was. The Mason-Dixon line dated back to the 1700s. Originally drawn as the border between Pennsylvania and Maryland, it eventually came to separate the free states and slave states."

"Why is that important?" Jamal wondered.

"Because the treatment of African-Americans was quite a bit worse below the Mason-Dixon line. Many African-Americans growing up in the North or the Midwest were just not prepared for the more restrictive conditions of life in the South. Their first introduction to Jim Crow laws often happened right here in Washington, D.C., our nation's capital, where they received a rude awakening. When they arrived here by train, the first thing that they had to do was move to the Jim Crow car, reserved for blacks. They were no longer allowed to ride in the railroad cars that carried white passengers. As soon as they reached Tuskegee, they were treated to what the Air Corps called 'common-sense lectures.' These lectures were intended to make the men aware of conditions in the South, where

Jim Crow laws, segregation, lynchings, poll taxes, and other forms of racism were normal.

"You know, the really ironic thing was that while African-Americans tried to enter the flight-training program and were often rejected solely because they were black, the War Department was actively recruiting flight candidates. The Air Corps frequently held rallies, printed recruiting posters, and ran full-page advertisements in the newspapers looking for men to become part of the program. They were, of course, looking for white men, not black men. When the Air Corps was finally opened to African-Americans, the waiting list for the coveted training positions was so long that many qualified men had little or no hope of ever actually entering the flight-training program at Tuskegee."

"What happened to those men, Mr. Kennedy?"

"They were usually drafted into the army, Marcus.

"Months passed and the black pilots and crews remained at Tuskegee, where they trained and trained some more. Everyone openly questioned whether the 99th would ever make it to Europe. There were occasional rumors that orders were about to be issued for the transfer of the 99th Fighter Squadron for overseas duty, but that's all they were—just rumors.

"On April 2, 1943, after several false alarms, the men assigned to the 99th finally left Tuskegee Army Air Field and headed for Europe. After traveling by train to New York, four hundred members of the 99th Fighter Squadron shipped out aboard the SS *Mariposa*. Their next stop would be North Africa. They were finally headed for the war."

As the bell started to ring, announcing the end of the class, Mrs. Riggs appeared in the doorway. She was just in time to hear Victor Kennedy say, "That's all we have time for today, class. If you're still interested, we can talk about more of the story tomorrow."

She was pleasantly surprised to see that the students looked excited about the prospect of another lesson.

Chapter Three

Shipping Out

When the class resumed the next day, one of the students had a question. "Mr. Kennedy, we're talking about pilots here. Isn't that right?"

"Yes, pilots but also several hundred non-pilots, Luis. Remember, yesterday we talked a little bit about the support personnel—the men that kept the planes flying, cooked the food, built landing fields—all of them."

"Okay, Mr. Kennedy, I remember. But if there were pilots and they had airplanes, then why didn't they just fly everybody to Africa?"

"Well, just think about it. There were a couple of really big problems. What were they?" Several hands shot up. Kennedy pointed to a girl in the back of the room.

"Because back then, airplanes couldn't fly as far or as fast as they can today. Isn't that right?"

"That's right, Tiffany. Today, all of you are used to the idea of just getting on an airplane and, in a few hours, being almost anywhere in the world. But as you just said, in the 1940s, airplanes couldn't fly as far and certainly not as fast as the jet airplanes of today. They were so much smaller, only holding fifty or sixty passengers at the most, and not nearly as comfortable. So military personnel going off to war in Europe or the Pacific had to go by ships."

"But that was comfortable, wasn't it, Mr. Kennedy?" asked Makayla.

"No, it really wasn't. I guess some of you may have had the opportunity to go on a cruise ship with your parents or have at least watched a television show or a movie mentioning cruises. These ships weren't anything close to being like that. The transport ships were crowded with men and equipment—really crowded. Also, there was danger from German submarines that patrolled the Atlantic Ocean. For protection, several ships would travel together in convoys. Plus, the weather in the North Atlantic was frequently stormy."

"How long did a trip across the ocean take back then, Mr. Kennedy?"

"Usually a couple of weeks, Pham. Many of the men got seasick, the food wasn't very good, and don't forget the enemy submarines. By the time the men finally got to Europe or North Africa, they were very glad to set foot on land."

Charlene had another question. "Mr. Kennedy, how many people were on the ship?"

"There were about four thousand men on the SS *Mariposa,* a troop ship that could carry men and equipment back and forth across the ocean."

"Mr. Kennedy, how many of the men on the ship were black?"

"Only about four hundred, Jamal; the rest were white. Let me tell you something very remarkable about that trip: Lieutenant Colonel Benjamin O. Davis, Jr., was in charge of all of the men—both black and white—onboard the ship."

"What was so special about that? My father's in the army, and he's black, and he's got a lot of white guys that work for him."

"Well, Jamal," Kennedy responded, "that just shows you how far we've come, doesn't it? Back in 1943, it was unheard of for a black officer to be in charge of white men. It just wasn't done, and here on this one ship, we had Lieutenant Colonel Davis in charge of more than three thousand white men. It was just extraordinary. Let me try to put this into perspective for you. I hate to keep hammering away at this, but it's really important. What kind of society was America back then?" On cue, thirty students hollered out in unison:

"Segregated!"

"Very good! That's right, the United States was a segregated society where, in many places, African-Americans couldn't eat in restaurants with white people, ride in the same car on the train, or even try on clothing in a store. Blacks were expected to be subservient to whites. You know, mind their manners and stay in their place. So just think about it. For three weeks, an African-American was in charge of several thousand white soldiers. Let me tell you something else: Benjamin O. Davis, Jr., was the first African-American in the twentieth century to graduate from the United States Military Academy at West Point, New York. During the entire four years that he was there, unless it was on official business, none of the white cadets would talk to him. When he was a young man, probably about your age, on at least one occasion, he found himself face to face with an angry mob of Ku Klux Klan members who obviously had no use for black people. So this was really a very big deal."

"Mr. Kennedy, were there any problems onboard the ship? I mean, did Lieutenant Colonel Davis or the other black men have trouble with the white men, since the African-Americans were so much in the minority?"

"Well, there weren't any obvious problems or direct insubordination. Remember that this was the army, Marcus, and soldiers had to obey those in charge, no matter how much they might have hated the situation. There definitely was a lot of complaining and grumbling, however. Most white men weren't used to being so close to blacks— and vice versa. It was a very unusual situation; that's for sure. But it worked, and three weeks later, they all arrived safely in North Africa—Casablanca, Morocco, to be exact."

"Now it was time to go after the enemy. Right, Mr. Kennedy?" Pham and the rest of the class were ready for action.

"It wasn't quite that easy. The Army Air Corps wasn't any more ready for black pilots in Africa or Europe than they had been in America. Segregation was still a way of life and things weren't about to change, even in war. The men of the 99th Fighter Squadron were kept segregated. They lived in tents on one side of the air base while the white personnel were housed on the other side. There was very little interaction. Their paths really didn't cross very often."

"Mr. Kennedy, are you telling us that all of the whites ignored the black pilots and crewmembers? Didn't they have anything to do with them?" Makayla wondered.

"That's a really good question. You know, the truth of the matter lies somewhere in between. Since the men of the 99th lived in a separate area of the base, there just weren't a lot of reasons for blacks and whites to come in contact with each other, at least at the enlisted man's level. Everyone was kept pretty busy finishing the airfields and training for combat, so there wasn't much time for socializing. But, of course, there were occasional exceptions, such as when a couple of friendly white fighter pilots who had also made the trip across the Atlantic Ocean on the SS *Mariposa* visited the base. While there were some instances of friendship such as that, for the most part, the black pilots and crews of the 99th Fighter Squadron lived separate lives from the rest of the military personnel."

"Mr. Kennedy, when did the black pilots finally get into the war?" Pham asked.

"After being in North Africa for about a month, Lieutenant Colonel Davis and the 99th Fighter Squadron were transferred to a nearby base called Fardjouna. There, they were assigned to the 33rd Fighter Group, commanded by Colonel William Momyer. That was very unfortunate since Colonel Momyer really didn't want the 99th Fighter Squadron under his command. But that's a story we'll save for a little later.

"For several weeks, the job of the 99th was to go after Italian gun emplacements on Pantelleria Island, off the coast of Sicily. Each day, the pilots would fly their P-40 airplanes over Pantelleria and drop their five-hundred-pound bombs on the assigned targets."

"Were these dangerous missions, Mr. Kennedy?"

"Of course they were dangerous, Makayla. Those guns they were assigned to bomb were aimed right at them, trying to shoot them out of the air."

"Mr. Kennedy, when did the 99th finally get to fly with the bombers? Didn't they do that, too?" asked Marcus.

"You all know more about the Tuskegee Airmen than you let on, don't you?" Sheepish snickers filled the room.

"After flying lots of the kinds of missions where they went after gun emplacements and other ground targets, they finally got what they had been wanting for so long—a chance to make a *real* contribution to the war effort, an opportunity to meet the enemy in the air. After all, they had trained for that type of combat for a very long time.

"June 9, 1943, was a very important day for the black pilots from Tuskegee. They were finally assigned to fly bomber-escort missions for a group of American bombers that were going to attack Pantelleria. Thirteen planes from the 99th were protecting a dozen Douglas A-20s as they dropped their bombs over the target and headed home. Suddenly, four German Messerschmitt Me-109s attacked the bombers. In response, five of the 99th pilots headed their planes toward the Germans."

"Hooray," came a cheer in unison from the teenagers.

"No, there's no hooray here. There's nothing to cheer about," said Kennedy.

"But," asked Charlene, "isn't that what they wanted? Isn't that what they'd been waiting for all that time?"

"Yes, it was," said Kennedy, "but it wasn't what they were supposed to do. Their job was to stay with the bombers and provide protection, not fly off and try to shoot down enemy fighter planes. I told you about Colonel Momyer earlier. Well, he would soon use this incident to attempt to have the 99th Fighter Squadron removed from combat. He would argue that the black pilots couldn't follow orders. But we'll talk more about that a little later.

"At least for now, the pilots of the 99th Fighter Squadron were doing what they had been trained to do. Almost every day, the pilots flew bomber-escort missions, frequently sighting enemy aircraft and even getting into dogfights with the Germans on a couple of occasions."

"Mr. Kennedy, did they ever shoot any of the enemy fighters down?"

"It took about a month of combat before that happened, Luis. It was not until July 2, 1943, that one of the pilots of the 99th Fighter Squadron finally shot down a German airplane."

"Hooray," the class shouted. "Finally, something good!"

"Class, let me make something very clear. I'm not trying to glorify war here. Just the idea of war is horrible. The reality is even worse: homes are destroyed, and people are wounded or killed. World War II was horrible, but it was so very necessary to stop the Axis powers—Italy, Germany, and Japan—in their efforts to take over the whole world. Combat wasn't a video game at the arcade; it was something very serious and very dangerous. A lot of men and women lost their lives—on both sides.

"The first member of the 99th Fighter Squadron to shoot down a German airplane was Charles B. Hall of Brazil, Indiana. It happened while American bombers were on a mission near Sicily. When they were attacked by a large number of German Messerschmitt and Focke-Wulf airplanes, the order was given for the pilots of the 99th to go after them. And they did! When the Germans attacked, Lieutenant Charles Hall flew his plane out to meet them. As he neared the enemy airplanes, he began firing his machine guns at the first Focke-Wulf that approached him. Hall was a good shot. His bullets hit the German airplane, causing it to catch fire and fall toward the ground in an out-of-control spin. Hall also partially damaged a second German airplane, a Messerschmitt Me-109.

"That day, Charles Hall was very, very lucky to have returned to base safely. He ran into all kinds of trouble. A pair of German fighters that obviously wanted to shoot him down followed him the whole time he was trying to get back to the base. One of the German Messerschmitts would fly at him while the other hung back waiting for Hall to make his break. To make things worse, Lieutenant Hall's P-40 was getting low on gas. The Germans weren't about to let him get away. Hall radioed for help while his attackers kept at him, just waiting for the right range to shoot him down.

"Finally, Hall saw a pair of aircraft coming to his assistance—or so he thought. They turned out to be two German Focke-Wulf airplanes. Now, he had not two, but four German pilots that wanted to shoot him down." As Kennedy told the story, he could tell that the class was hanging on each word, anxiously waiting for the next. Through Kennedy's retelling of Hall's attempts to escape the attacking Germans, the class relived the story, almost as if they were part of the action.

"What'd he do, Mr. Kennedy, what'd he do?" they called out in unison.

"What'd he do, what'd he do?" echoed Kennedy with a smile on his face. "What he did was be patient, use his brain, and remember what he'd been taught. For almost twenty minutes, Charles Hall put his P-40 through a series of evasive maneuvers that had been drilled into him at Tuskegee.

"Now do you see the value of a good education and hard work?" the teacher asked. The class groaned, and Kennedy couldn't resist a smile.

"He got back safely, didn't he, Mr. Kennedy?" Makayla was obviously worried.

"Once he got away from the Germans, Hall thought he was home safe." As the class stood and applauded, Kennedy burst their bubble.

"But he wasn't, not yet. Nearing base, he ran into a group of Allied bombers and moved in to join them. Unfortunately for Hall, they mistook him for an enemy fighter plane and prepared to shoot him down. Hall turned his airplane around and, once again, found himself the object of some very unwanted attention. Finally, he was able to radio his identity, and the American fighters gave up their chase. Hall was, at last, able to land after a very harrowing adventure." Smiles broke out on thirty young faces as Kennedy finished his story.

"But there's something that I need to tell you. A very lucky Charles Hall became the first African-American pilot to shoot down an enemy fighter, but there's more to this story. Two of Lieutenant Hall's fellow pilots died that day. Sherman White and James McCullin were the first two members of the 99th Fighter Squadron to die in combat. It was a very bittersweet day for the 99th. There was tremendous joy—and tremendous sadness. That was what war was like." The smiles immediately disappeared from the thirty faces. The excitement that had surged through their bodies earlier disappeared just as quickly. It was almost as if a door had been opened, allowing all of their happy emotions to escape.

"I want you to understand something. War is not pretty. War is horrible and it is for real, not like a television show, a movie, or even a video game. There's no rewind button. You can't change the horrible things and make them turn out the way you want."

"Mr. Kennedy, what happened after that?" Pham inquired.

"For the next several weeks, life continued on pretty much as it had before. Almost every day, unless the weather was bad, the mechanics would get the airplanes ready, and the pilots would fly their missions—sometimes as many as two or three each day. The missions were all pretty much the same, since it was now the job of the 99th Fighter Squadron to protect the bombers from enemy aircraft. They'd fly from the base to an assigned point where they'd meet the American bombers and then escort them to and from the targets. All the while, they had to stay alert for German fighters, plus worry about the antiaircraft artillery fire coming at them from the ground. That was really their worst concern, the very deadly German antiaircraft fire that they couldn't control. Enemy airplanes were dangerous, of course, but the American fighter pilots were well trained. One on one with a German attacker, well, that was considered an even match. But the antiaircraft fire was a whole different matter—very scary and very deadly!"

"Mr. Kennedy, were the pilots scared? I know I'd be." Luis admitted.

"Scared is probably not quite the way to describe what they felt. Of course, there had to be a certain amount of apprehension. Each of these men knew what they were up against. They knew the risks, but they also knew that they were well prepared. They had trained for a long time, and they all wanted to be where they were. But, of course, there was fear. For anybody who goes into war and puts his or her life on the line, there's got to be some fear. It's only natural."

"Mr. Kennedy, was the 99th Fighter Squadron the only group of black fighter pilots during the war?"

"No, it wasn't. There were three other fighter squadrons—the 100th, 301st, and the 302nd. Remember that I told you as the training continued at Tuskegee Army Air Field, more pilots graduated and needed a place to go. The 99th couldn't absorb them all, and they obviously couldn't be assigned to white squadrons, so the Air Corps activated three additional African-American fighter squadrons. Those three squadrons formed the 332nd Fighter Group. Since Lieutenant Colonel Davis had done a great job in charge of the 99th, the Air Corps sent him back to the United States and reassigned him as commanding officer of the 332nd."

A hand went up in the back of the room. "Mr. Kennedy, does that mean that the black fliers were accepted? That their accomplishments were finally being recognized?"

"Sadly, the answer is no. Lieutenant Colonel Davis was a very strong commander, and when he returned to the United States, there were some people that thought this was the perfect opportunity to attack the reputation and the accomplishments of the 99th Fighter Squadron."

"Mr. Kennedy, why would anyone want to do that? It sounds like the black pilots were doing a really good job."

"The pilots and the support personnel had done a marvelous job, Tiffany, and everyone should've been proud of them. Certainly African-Americans in the United States were. On a weekly basis, their accomplishments were written about in African-American newspapers such as the *Chicago Defender* and the *Pittsburgh Courier*. But in the major newspapers, their accomplishments were pretty much ignored.

"But it's important to remember that the leadership of the military was simply a reflection of American society in general. And, of course, as we all know, back then, America was . . ."

"SEGREGATED!"

"That's right, American society was a segregated society, so it only stands to reason that for the most part, the military was also segregated. And many, but certainly not all, of the leaders in the military, as well as in the government, wanted to keep the military segregated."

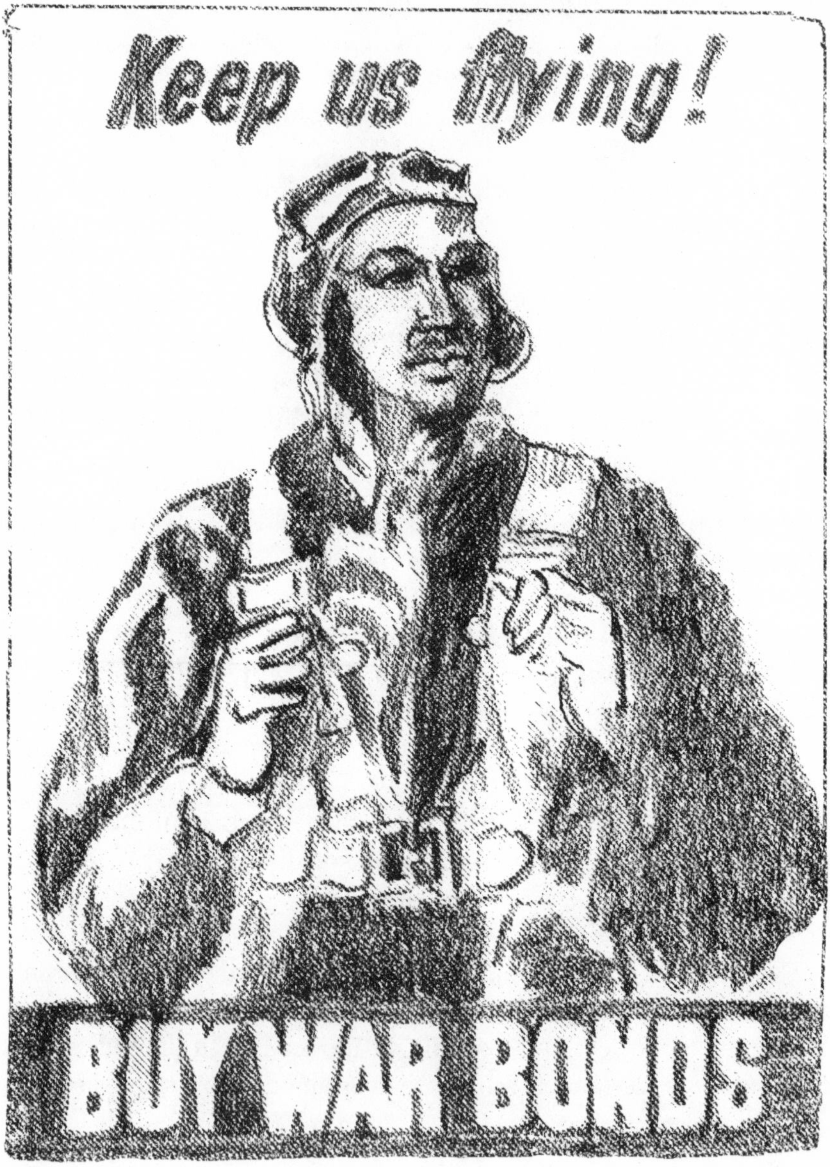
Keep us flying!
BUY WAR BONDS

Chapter Four

Proving Themselves

"As I started to tell you, as soon as Lieutenant Colonel Davis returned to the United States, several people in the military decided that the time was right to undo all of the good things that the 99th Fighter Squadron had done."

"What happened?"

"Who did it?"

"That wasn't fair." Questions and comments rang out across the room.

"Do you remember I had told you earlier about Colonel Momyer?" Heads nodded. "When the 99th first arrived in Africa, they were assigned to the 33rd Fighter Group, commanded by Colonel Momyer, who didn't want them. After Lieutenant Colonel Davis left, Colonel Momyer reported that the progress and accomplishments of the 99th had been less than satisfactory. In his official report to one of the generals, Momyer claimed that the African-American pilots had neither the proper motivation nor discipline. He said that in combat, when the 99th Fighter Squadron's pilots met the enemy, the black pilots scattered. In effect, what Momyer seemed to be saying was that the black pilots were cowards and afraid to face the enemy. Momyer hoped that the 99th would be assigned to a non-combatant role and that the 332nd Fighter Group that was still in training in the United States would never be assigned to combat in Europe."

"What happened then?" Marcus asked.

"You all know what happens when a rumor gets started, don't you?" Heads nodded. "What happens?" asked Kennedy.

"It spreads all over, even if it makes no sense. Even if it's a bunch of lies," said a student.

"But people believe it anyway," said someone else.

"That's right," said Kennedy, "and that's exactly what happened in this case. The things that were said about the 99th Fighter Squadron were certainly not true, but by the time enough people had heard them and repeated them . . . well, you know what happens."

"Yes," the students chimed in, "people start to believe them."

"This report got so far out of hand that it became very serious. Major news publications started to question the ability of African-Americans to fight in combat and argued that commanders didn't want them. It became a very weighty issue, and it all boiled down to whether or not black soldiers had the ability to be as good as white soldiers.

"Fortunately, a lot of people argued very strongly against Colonel Momyer's charges and the immediate damage was finally undone. But you all know what sometimes happens when you're accused of doing something wrong, even if it's not true, don't you?"

"Sure," they all shouted out, "everyone thinks you're guilty anyway!"

"Eventually, an official report came out disagreeing with what Colonel Momyer had claimed; it stated that the 99th Fighter Squadron was just as good as any other squadron. But damage had been done and the reputation of the 99th had been tarnished through no fault of its own. And that's just an idea of the kinds of things that African-Americans faced for wanting to be part of their country's military."

"Mr. Kennedy, were all of the white commanders like that Colonel Momyer guy? I mean, did they all want to get rid of the pilots from Tuskegee?"

"You know, Jamal, sometimes it must seem that way. But the answer is no, they were not. In October 1943, the 99th Fighter Squadron was transferred to Foggia Air Field on the east coast of

Italy. They became part of the 79th Fighter Group under the command of Colonel Earl Bates. Unlike Momyer, Colonel Bates welcomed the black pilots to the 79th Fighter Group.

"Class, how do you behave, how do you perform when you know that you're welcome? When you know that someone likes and respects you? When you know that someone has confidence in you and trusts you?" Several hands went up.

"You work harder."

"It makes you feel good."

"I want to make them proud of me."

"You are all right. All of those things are correct, and I imagine that's how the men of the 99th must've felt when they knew that Colonel Bates was glad to have them around.

"That's when their reputation really started to grow. They really started to prove themselves to others. They already knew how capable they were. Now it was the time and place to show others what they could do. It wasn't really that they were any different. What had really changed was that Colonel Bates gave them the opportunity, when Colonel Momyer had done just the opposite."

"Mr. Kennedy, were they in more battles? Did the black pilots shoot down more of the enemy?"

"Yes, Pham, they did. By the time the war ended, the African-American pilots from the 99th Fighter Squadron and the 332nd Fighter Group shot down a total of one hundred and eleven enemy aircraft."

"All right!" shouted a boy in the back of the classroom.

"It was certainly quite an accomplishment," continued Kennedy, "but I want you to keep in mind that the cost was not cheap. Over the course of World War II, during combat, sixty-six black pilots were killed and another thirty-two became prisoners of war.

"I know that you're interested in some of the battles, and I don't blame you. They were exciting, but please keep in mind that this wasn't Hollywood. This was the real thing—where people lost their lives.

"Certainly two of the most successful days in the war for the 99th Fighter Squadron took place on January 27 and 28 of 1944. Over these two days, the African-American pilots destroyed twelve enemy aircraft and damaged several others. In fact, a couple of the pilots shot down two German aircraft each. Robert Deiz, who eventually went on to pose for a war bond poster titled 'Keep Us Flying,' was one of the pilots. Charles Hall also shot down two enemy airplanes. Does anyone remember Charles Hall?" Hands shot up throughout the room.

"He was the first black pilot to shoot down an enemy fighter."

"That's right," Kennedy agreed. "Several months earlier, Charles Hall had become the first black pilot to shoot down an enemy airplane."

"They did good, Mr. Kennedy. Didn't they?"

"They sure did," said Kennedy. "Their achievements that day were certainly noteworthy. They definitely caught the attention of a lot of people, but there might have been something even more important."

Luis demanded, "What's that, Mr. Kennedy?"

"Attitudes were changing," Kennedy told the students. "Do you remember that I told you how the effectiveness of the 99th had been challenged by the military and some of the major newspapers just a few months earlier? Now, *Time* magazine seemed to be one of the biggest supporters of the black pilots. The magazine told its readers, 'Any outfit would have been proud of the combat excellence of one of the most controversial outfits in the Army.' After that, when people talked about the 99th Fighter Squadron, they talked about how well trained, confident, and brave the African-Americans were.

"Things were improving, to be sure. Many of the leaders in the military were changing their tunes. Originally, the commander of the Army Air Forces, General Henry Arnold, had been opposed to the formation of a black fighter squadron. With this new attitude, however, when he spoke about the 99th Fighter Squadron, he was complimentary."

"Mr. Kennedy, when did the other squadrons of black pilots go to war?"

"Charlene, it was almost a year after the arrival of the 99th Fighter Squadron. In January and February of 1944, the 332nd Fighter Group, commanded by Lieutenant Colonel Benjamin O. Davis, Jr., arrived in Italy, at a base just south of Naples. It didn't take long before they were seeing action. Their assignments were very similar to what the 99th Fighter Squadron was doing. They provided protection for American bombers and flew lots of reconnaissance missions.

"I know you like action, so here goes. The pilots of the 332nd Fighter Group had a very rewarding day on June 9, 1944. They shot down five German airplanes while they were providing protection for a group of American bombers assigned targets in Udine, Italy. As the bombers approached the target, several German Messerschmitt aircraft suddenly attacked them. Frederick Funderburg quickly fired at one of the attacking enemy Me-109s. His aim was deadly. The German airplane shuddered from the impact of machine-gun fire, and then it exploded. Only seconds later, Funderburg shot a second German aircraft out of the air.

"Wendell Pruitt maneuvered around behind one of the Germans. There was no way the Messerschmitt was going to escape. Pruitt fired his machine guns as the German pilot tried to evade streams of deadly bullets. As the wing of the German Messerschmitt erupted in flames, the pilot climbed out and parachuted to the earth.

"Charles Bussey went after a Messerschmitt Me-109. He fired his machine guns while the German pilot maneuvered in an attempt to get away. Bussey kept firing, hitting the Me-109's tail and crippling the airplane. The German pilot managed to escape only by parachuting to safety. His empty airplane screamed toward the ground and exploded on impact.

"The enemy had nearly shot down Melvin Jackson, a pilot nicknamed 'Red' because of his red hair and almost white complexion. Fortunately, Charles Bussey had just shot down the German that had Jackson in his sights. Jackson then was able to go after one of the German aircraft and destroy it!

"I know you want to cheer, so go ahead." The entire class immediately stood up and erupted into cheers. "This was a very important mission for the 332nd Fighter Group. It was really their baptism under fire and they had done a marvelous job. Lieutenant Colonel Davis received the Distinguished Flying Cross as a result of this mission. They were finally being recognized for their accomplishments.

Perhaps just as important, one of the white bomber pilots involved with the mission paid them the supreme compliment. He reported, 'Your formation flying and escort is the best we have ever seen.' Unfortunately, the success of the mission had been offset by the death of Lieutenant Cornelius Rogers."

"Mr. Kennedy, I don't understand this squadron, group, and wing thing that you talk about. What's it mean?"

"It's simply a means of organization, Tiffany. A squadron is the basic unit, which is made up of airplanes and men. Three or four squadrons comprise a group, and finally, several groups make up a wing. You know, like you have one student. That student is part of a class. The class is part of the school and the school is part of a school district—just a means of organizing things.

"But while we're talking about squadrons and groups, this is a good time to talk about a very important event. Remember that the 99th Fighter Squadron was part of the 79th Fighter Group. The other African-American squadrons were part of—"

"I know. I know the answer," called out a girl in the front row.

"What do you know?" asked Kennedy.

"I know that the three squadrons of the 332nd Fighter Group were the 100th, 301st, and 302nd Fighter Squadrons."

"That's right," said Kennedy. "You've been paying attention. Now, keep in mind, these two organizations of African-American pilots, the 99th Fighter Squadron and the 332nd Fighter Group were not together. They were assigned to different organizations. In fact, the 99th was flying as part of an integrated unit since the other squadrons in the 79th Fighter Group were made up of white pilots."

"Well, that was a good thing. Wasn't it, Mr. Kennedy?" asked Makayla.

"It certainly was. The 99th was doing a very good job. They were flying as part of a white fighter group, and most importantly, they were being accepted for *what* they were."

"What was that, Mr. Kennedy? What were they?"

"They were a well-trained fighter squadron that was just as capable as any other group of men, Jamal. It didn't matter whether they were black or white. What really mattered was that they were good. Race didn't matter.

"I've already told you that the 332nd was also now in Europe. Well, on July 3, 1944, the 99th Fighter Squadron became a part of the 332nd Fighter Group. Now, the 332nd had four squadrons, the 99th, 100th, 301st, and 302nd, under the command of recently promoted Colonel Benjamin O. Davis, Jr."

"That was a good thing. Right, Mr. Kennedy?"

"No, not really, Makayla," said Kennedy. "The 332nd Fighter Group was now an exception, something different, for several reasons. Fighter groups were normally made up of three squadrons, but now the 332nd had four squadrons. Also, since everyone in the 332nd was an African-American, it was a segregated unit. The 99th had been a well-functioning and accepted part of an integrated fighter group. Obviously, many of the men felt like they were now taking a step backwards."

"Mr. Kennedy, you've told us about several of the missions where the fighter pilots would fly with the bombers to keep the Germans from shooting the bombers down. What I want to know is, how many airplanes would normally take part in one of these missions?"

"That's a very good question, Luis, but the answer varies. Let me tell you about one particular mission that took place on July 12, 1944. It was a mission that included forty-two airplanes flown by pilots from the 100th, 301st, and 302nd Fighter Squadrons. Their job that day was to provide protection for a group of B-24 bombers on a mission to France.

"As the bombers and the fighter airplanes got close to their assigned target, enemy fighters were spotted in the distance, but they didn't appear to be a threat. The bombers dropped their bombs and everyone was preparing to head for home. More enemy fighters were seen, but again, they were pretty far away and didn't seem to be a problem.

"All of a sudden, six enemy airplanes headed toward the bomber formation. The Americans, bomber pilots and fighter pilots alike, were shooting at the German pilots as they attacked the bombers. Almost immediately, two of the German Focke-Wulf Fw-190s were shot down. At the same time, from another position, sixteen more Fw-190s headed for the bombers, intent on shooting them down. Several of the black pilots headed toward the Germans to keep them away from the American bombers.

"Joseph Elsberry almost immediately had one of the German airplanes in his gun sights. Things were happening really fast. As soon as Elsberry shot down the German plane, another crossed in front of him. Elsberry started firing at that German, and the attacker quickly attempted to escape. He never got away, as Elsberry's machine-gun fire raked the Focke-Wulf. The German airplane crashed and burned.

"Think about Joseph Elsberry's excitement when he looked to the side and spied another German aircraft as a target. As Elsberry opened fire, the German tried to get away. When the Focke-Wulf Fw-190 plunged into an uncontrollable dive, the enemy plane smashed into the ground.

"Just imagine, Joseph Elsberry had shot down three enemy airplanes on one mission. He was the first black pilot to do that."

"Go Elsberry!" shouted the class.

"You know, only eight days later, Joseph Elsberry shot down yet another enemy airplane. Now, he had four enemy airplanes to his credit."

"Go man, go," they cried out.

"Obviously, you're all very interested in the battles and the dogfights. I don't blame you—the stories are exciting. July 18, 1944, was one of the most successful days in the air for the pilots. This was a four-squadron mission. By this time, the 332nd had received the P-51 Mustang, which was a highly maneuverable and very fast airplane. Anyway, that morning, almost seventy P-51s took off. Their assignment was to cover the bombers into Germany as they went after the Memmingen Airdrome, or airfield.

"As was true with so many of these missions, it was common to see dozens of enemy aircraft in the distance. On this mission, the Germans were close. They planned to attack the bombers, but it wasn't going to be easy since the Tuskegee Airmen were protecting them. Near the target, the formation of American bombers and fighter aircraft spotted a large number of German aircraft off to their right side."

"Exactly what is a large number, Mr. Kennedy? How many German airplanes were there?"

"A lot, Pham. Probably about thirty-five. As the Americans flew on, the Germans separated into smaller units of anywhere from two to five airplanes. Then they attacked. They flew in from slightly above and slightly below the American airplanes. That was a big mistake. The African-American pilots were ready for them. Within minutes, the fighter pilots from Tuskegee shot nine Messerschmitt Me-109s out of the sky.

"The convoy of American airplanes continued toward their target. They still had a job to finish. Flying at an altitude of about twenty-six thousand feet, they caught sight of another large group of enemy airplanes, both Focke-Wulf and Messerschmitt aircraft. As the bombers flew on, the Germans followed them, keeping out of range of the P-51 Mustangs' machine guns.

"Four of the Focke-Wulf Fw-190s gained altitude, flying about a thousand feet higher than the American airplanes. Suddenly, the four Germans sped toward the bombers, hoping for an easy kill. It wasn't going to happen. The pilots of the 332nd Fighter Group headed for the Germans. Two P-51 pilots quickly maneuvered their Mustangs behind a pair of German Fw-190s and began firing their machine guns. Two of the enemy aircraft soon fell victim to the guns of the American airplanes. The other two Germans quickly turned tail and got away.

"It had been a very successful day for the 332nd Fighter Group. Eleven enemy aircraft had been shot down. Lee Archer, Charles Bailey, Roger Romine, Walter Palmer, Edward Toppins, and Hugh Warner had each shot down one German airplane. Jack Holsclaw shot down a pair of Messerschmitts. Clarence Lester was credited with the destruction of three German airplanes. By the way, Clarence Lester's nickname was 'Lucky'. I guess it's pretty obvious why."

Chapter Five

There Were Bombers, Too

"Well, class, what do you think of the Tuskegee Airmen so far?" asked Kennedy. Several hands rose around the classroom.

"Mr. Kennedy, they were great. They were really, really heroes."

"That's true," said Kennedy. "They were great. And, in many cases, they certainly were heroes. But what do you know about them? You've heard me telling you about some of their stories, some of their accomplishments. But what I really want to know is, what do you know about them?" Kennedy was met by blank stares. Some of the students scratched their heads.

"I guess my question is not very clear," said Kennedy. "Who were the Tuskegee Airmen?" he asked. This time, several students waved their hands, sure that they knew the answer.

"Yes?" responded Kennedy to one of the more eager pupils.

"Well," said the young man, "they were black men, and they flew airplanes."

"That's right," agreed Kennedy. "They were black men and they flew airplanes. But what kinds of airplanes did they fly?"

"Fighter planes!" shouted out the class in unison.

"How do you know they flew fighter planes?" asked Kennedy.

"You told us that, Mr. Kennedy. Don't you remember?" asked Pham.

"I remember, but they also flew bomber airplanes," said Kennedy.

"In the war?" asked one of the students.

"During the war," said Kennedy, "but not in the war."

"Well, Mr. Kennedy, isn't that the same? What do you mean?" Luis demanded.

"Let me tell you," said Kennedy. "I told you earlier about the difficulties that African-Americans first had when they wanted to be in the Army Air Corps. As I keep saying, America was a segregated society and the army didn't want blacks in the Air Corps. But, as you know by now, it eventually happened and the all-black fighter squadrons finally came into being.

"Many African-American organizations, such as the NAACP, labor unions, political groups, and as always, the black newspapers, kept pushing for inclusion. Of course, they wanted blacks flying fighter airplanes, but they also wanted African-Americans to have the opportunity to fly bombers. And that eventually happened as well."

"That was a good thing, wasn't it, Mr. Kennedy?"

"That was a very good thing, class," said Kennedy, "but it was also a very hard struggle full of difficulties. In mid-1943, the military activated the 477th Bombardment Group."

"Mr. Kennedy, what's activated mean?" questioned Tiffany.

"It means that the group was started, that's all. It's just a military term. Anyway, plans called for the 477th to be manned entirely by African-Americans. This was certainly a major achievement, but it was still not what a lot of black people in America wanted."

"Why not, Mr. Kennedy?"

"Well, Marcus, they really wanted an end to segregation. They wanted the government to integrate the military, but they had to settle for Air Corps units such as the 477th Bombardment Group and the 332nd Fighter Group. Of course, these groups were still segregated."

"Mr. Kennedy, what was the 477th going to do?" asked Charlene. "I mean, what was their job going to be?"

"The army planned to have the 477th fly bombers. By the time the group was fully trained, there would be almost twelve hundred African-American men who would be able to fly and maintain sixty B-25 twin-engine bombers. Depending on how the war was going, they might be sent either to Europe to fight the Germans or to the Pacific to battle the Japanese."

"Did the 99th Fighter Squadron or the 332nd Fighter Group ever get to protect the bombers of the 477th Bombardment Group during the war?" asked another student.

"No," said Kennedy, "but that is a really good question. Unfortunately, the answer is no because the 477th Bombardment Group never had the chance to become part of the war."

"Why not?" cried the students in one voice.

"It's a long story. Are you sure that you want to hear it?" teased Kennedy.

"Yes, yes!" the class hollered.

"Well, I think that the military simply did not want African-Americans gaining any more footholds in the armed forces than they already had," said Kennedy.

"Throughout the years, the government had undertaken several studies concerning the ability of blacks to function as part of the military. The reports supposedly proved that African-Americans were just not fit to be part of the Air Corps because they lacked either the mental or physical capacity that was required. Of course, the studies were always incorrect, but the government still used the results as a way to keep African-Americans out of the Army Air Corps."

"That's bogus," yelled out one boy in the back of the room.

"That was very bogus, indeed," agreed Kennedy. "But it's what happened. One report stated, 'It is common knowledge that the colored race does not have the technical nor the flying background for the creation of a bombardment-type unit.' And, you know, there was some truth to that statement." Hands quickly went up throughout the room.

"Mr. Kennedy, how can you say that?" Jamal asked indignantly. "Are you agreeing with those reports?"

"Of course not," said Kennedy, "I'm an eighty-year-old black man. Do you think I would agree with statements like that? Do you think that I'd agree with a stupid study that concluded that the brain of a black man was smaller than that of a white man? Or that blacks lacked the bravery or commitment to excel in the military? Or that black people were lazy or shiftless? Do you think that I could agree with any of those foolish conclusions?" Kennedy challenged. Most of the class shook their heads. Marcus raised his hand.

"Yes?" said Kennedy.

"But, Mr. Kennedy, you said that there was truth to that statement about blacks having neither the technical nor the flying background."

"Well, of course there was," said Kennedy. "That report was a perfect example of a Catch-22. Does anyone know what a Catch-22 is?" One or two hands tentatively went up.

"A Catch-22 is something like when you want to get a job but nobody will hire you because you've never had a job before. So you can't get a job because you don't have any experience, but you can't get experience because you can't get a job."

"Luis, that's a very good explanation of a Catch-22," said Kennedy. "You see, that's exactly what that report meant. African-Americans didn't have the technical or flying background to fly military airplanes because they'd never been given the opportunity to learn. But, and this is very important, just because they hadn't been flying or working on military airplanes certainly didn't mean that they didn't have the ability to do so or that they shouldn't be given the opportunity to learn. However, people in the military erroneously believed that African-Americans didn't have the ability. So, you see, it's pretty evident that the cards were stacked against the 477th Bombardment Group before it ever got started. This is what the men faced.

"The bomber training was supposed to take place at Selfridge Field, Michigan. At least, that was going to be the home base of the 477th Bombardment Group. The pilot training still continued at Tuskegee Army Air Field. At a certain point in the program, the cadets were trained as either single-engine or twin-engine pilots. You know, for fighter or bomber aircraft. When their training was completed at Tuskegee, the twin-engine pilots were transferred to Selfridge."

A hand went up in the back of the class. Kennedy pointed toward the young girl and waited for her question.

"Mr. Kennedy, how many people were part of a bomber crew? And what did they do?"

"Well," said Kennedy, "a B-25 bomber crew was made up of six men. A B-25 required a pilot and a copilot who, of course, were responsible for flying the airplane. And there was also a navigator, a bombardier, and two gunners. The navigator's job was to plot the course, follow a map, if you will, and make sure the plane was flying in the right direction. The bombardier dropped the bombs on the targets. The gunners manned the weapons to defend against attacking enemy airplanes.

"But let's get back to the bomber training," continued Kennedy. "In a way, it was really a departure from the typical program at Tuskegee in that the men were being sent all over the country to learn their particular jobs. Various classes were held at airfields in Florida, Texas, New Mexico, Michigan, Illinois, Alabama, Nebraska, and even South Dakota. Pilots as well as ground crews also trained at several bases in California."

Tiffany appeared perplexed. "But, Mr. Kennedy, if the men were sent to all of those different bases, they must have been training with white men. I mean, you taught us that the only base that was just for African-Americans was Tuskegee. Isn't that right?"

"Yes, that's right, Tiffany," said Kennedy. "But while there might've been some training of blacks and whites together at these bases, for the most part, the living conditions would've been separate.

"Let me give you a specific example. When the African-American pilots were first sent to Mather Field in California, they were able to go anywhere on the base. There was no segregation and obviously they enjoyed that. Then one of the high-ranking generals visited the base and noticed that the black and white pilots were using the same facilities. Well, this general didn't like that, so he ordered Mather's commanding officer to segregate the base."

"That wasn't fair, Mr. Kennedy."

"No, Jamal," said Kennedy, "it definitely was not fair. And when it happened, the African-American pilots also didn't think it was very fair."

"What'd they do, Mr. Kennedy?"

"Well, you know, there really wasn't much they could do other than make a small protest. They decided that they would refuse to eat in a segregated dining hall. So they ate at the base's post exchange instead, even though it meant they had to pay for their meals out of their own pockets."

Makayla asked, "What's a post exchange, Mr. Kennedy?"

"It's kind of like a store," said Kennedy, "a small mall where military people would shop on the base.

"But let me tell you, class," said Kennedy, "that was just a small problem for the men in the 477th Bombardment Group. They had much bigger difficulties to contend with than that. In fact, they faced so many obstacles that it was almost as if the Air Corps was determined to make the program fail.

"The 477th Bombardment Group consisted of four squadrons: the 616th, 617th, 618th, and 619th. Although the group was intended to be all black, the original plan called for white officers to hold all positions of authority until the African-Americans had the experience and training to replace them. For that reason, Colonel Robert Selway, Jr., and other white officers were temporarily put in charge of the African-American bomber group.

"Unfortunately, it didn't turn out to be temporary. Colonel Selway did not want to give up control. He also didn't want to put African-American men in positions of authority. Selway was, without a doubt, a strong believer in segregation.

"And to make things worse, as part of a training program, the 477th was directly under the authority of the First Air Force, commanded by Major General Frank O. Hunter. General Hunter made the way he felt about African-Americans pretty clear. He believed in segregation and expressed the opinion that 'racial friction will occur if colored and white pilots are trained together.' On several occasions, General Hunter told African-American airmen that he would not tolerate any attempts to integrate military facilities. As I'm sure you can imagine, it was a very difficult situation for the men of the 477th Bombardment Group.

"Things did not go well for the 477th. Frequent problems caused the training to fall behind schedule. The group had a hard time keeping the desired number of men. Although the 477th was supposed to be ready for combat by November 1944, it wasn't going to happen then, if ever. As bad as things were at Selfridge Field in Michigan, they were only going to get worse as the days went by."

"Mr. Kennedy, how could things get worse?"

"Well, Charlene, the Air Corps kept transferring the men assigned to the 477th Bombardment Group from one base to another. And every base seemed to be worse than the last. After training at Selfridge Field for several months, the 477th was transferred to Godman Field, Kentucky. When the men openly questioned the reason for the transfer, the official answer was that Kentucky had better flying weather than Michigan. Most of the men believed that they had been transferred to a Southern state such as Kentucky because the treatment would be harsher. Many also believed that the government wanted to get the black men away from Selfridge Field because it was located too close to Detroit, home to a large number of African-Americans.

"In the middle of March 1945, the 477th Bombardment Group was transferred to Freeman Field in Indiana. The situation just kept getting worse. Not only were the African-American airmen unwelcome on the base, but they were also not wanted in the nearby town of Seymour. Of course, facilities on the base were segregated. In Seymour, although segregation was not the law, it was a fact of life. Laundries, grocery stores, restaurants, and other civilian facilities refused to serve African-Americans. The men certainly were not happy.

"Only a few weeks after the 477th arrived at Freeman Field, big trouble began. Only white personnel stationed at Freeman Field could use certain buildings on the base. The use of the officers' club became a real problem. Colonel Robert Selway prohibited African-Americans at Freeman Field from using the officers' club, known as Club Number Two. The club would be available for use only by people stationed at Freeman Field or for supervisory personnel." A hand quickly shot up.

"Mr. Kennedy, there's something I don't understand about what you just said."

"What's that, Marcus?" asked Kennedy.

"Weren't the African-American airmen stationed at Freeman Field?"

"Well, of course they were," agreed Kennedy. "And that's one thing that made Colonel Selway's order hard to understand. Selway argued that since the African-American airmen were there for training, they were not really stationed there. As trainees, they were not allowed to use the club. Doesn't make a lot of sense, does it? But that's not all. Certainly, some of the African-Americans at Freeman Field were supervisors of one kind or another. Therefore, they should've been allowed to use the officers' club, but Colonel Selway disagreed. Even worse, some of these men had already seen combat in Europe or had been in the military for quite some time. They should hardly have been classified as trainees." Another hand went up.

"Mr. Kennedy, I know why Colonel Selway did those things, why he gave those orders."

"Why?" asked Kennedy.

"It's simple," said Jamal, "he just didn't want African-Americans to be able to use the club. Isn't that so?"

"Bingo," said Kennedy, "you're exactly right. Colonel Selway really believed in segregation, and he was determined to make sure that his segregationist programs were followed. But," continued Kennedy, "these men did not intend to allow Colonel Selway to treat them like that."

"What did they do, Mr. Kennedy? What could they do?" asked Pham.

"What they did," answered Kennedy, "was take a very big chance. They decided to go against Colonel Selway's orders. They chose to fight against what they considered to be an injustice. They were going to go to the officers' club and use it. As a group, they decided that on a specific date, several of the men would visit the club in defiance of Selway's orders, but Colonel Selway had no intention of allowing that to happen."

"What'd he do, Mr. Kennedy?"

"He ordered military policemen to stand guard at the door of the officers' club and not allow any African-American airmen to enter." A sense of anxiety was building and several hands waved.

"What happened next, Mr. Kennedy? What happened?"

"Well, Makayla, on April 5, several black men tried to enter the club."

"Uh-oh," said several students.

"Uh-oh is right," agreed Kennedy. "Things were about to happen. Before the day ended, more than thirty African-American military officers were arrested."

"No!" shouted the class as one.

"And it wasn't going to stop there," Kennedy told the class, "it was going to get worse. The next day, twenty-four more black men headed for the officers' club. As soon as they walked into the building, they were also arrested.

"Two days later, all of the African-American officers who had been arrested were ordered released—all except for three."

"Mr. Kennedy, why were they all let go except for three?"

"Well, Tiffany, these three men, Marsden Thompson, Shirley Clinton, and Roger Terry, had been accused of an even greater crime than trying to go into the officers' club. They were accused of pushing white officers at the door when they were not allowed to enter.

"Colonel Selway was starting to worry a little. This was turning into a real problem for him. When it didn't look like it was going to get any better, he decided that he'd better talk to his boss, General Hunter, to find out what to do.

"What Colonel Selway and General Hunter decided to do did not make things better. In fact, it made things worse. They came up with a new regulation that said facilities were definitely going to be segregated. All officers at Freeman Field, whether they were black or white, had to read the new regulation. Then they had to sign a paper saying that they had read and understood the order.

"Well, class, guess what happened next?" No one volunteered a guess.

"One hundred and one African-American military officers refused to sign the paper. Selway was not happy about this. He kept at them. Each day the men were brought in and ordered to read the order and sign that they had read it. Each time this was done, they refused to sign. On April 12, 1945, Colonel Selway finally ordered all of the men arrested. The next day, they were rounded up, put on airplanes, and taken to Godman Field, where they remained under arrest." The class booed and hissed.

"Things were about to change. The top generals in the army quickly heard what was going on. Now, General Hunter and Colonel Selway found themselves in trouble."

"Yeah! All right!" the students cheered.

"The order came down for Hunter and Selway to release the 101 African-American officers. The charges against them would be dropped. General Hunter was not happy. He made it clear that he wasn't willing to release the men and he was not going to drop the charges. He was soon going to be a lot less happy. On April 21, the African-American officers were released."

"Free at last," shouted out one of the seventh graders, bringing laughs from everyone in the room, including Kennedy.

"A few weeks later, the entire 477th Bombardment Group was sent to Freeman Field to join the released members of their unit. I guess it's easy to understand that while the officers' club mess was a victory of sorts, the spirits of the group were not good. Lieutenants Thompson, Clinton, and Terry were still in jail, awaiting trial for pushing the white officers at the officers' club. Eventually, Marsden Thompson and Shirley Clinton were found not guilty. Roger Terry was not as fortunate. He was found guilty and fined. It was a conviction that he would carry on his record for the next fifty years until it was finally overturned in 1995.

"The resistance at Freeman Field had one very positive outcome for the men of the 477th Bombardment Group: Colonel Selway was forced to give up his command. On July 1, 1945, Colonel Benjamin O. Davis, Jr., returned home from Europe to become the new commander of the 477th Bombardment Group." The entire class stood up and applauded. With a smile on his face, Kennedy joined in the celebration. And on that happy note, the class ended for the day.

Chapter Six

A Long Way to Go

The next morning, Victor Kennedy resumed the story of the Tuskegee Airmen, saying, "Let's get back to the 332nd Fighter Group and the war in Europe. Do you remember that in July 1944 the 99th Fighter Squadron joined the three squadrons of the 332nd Fighter Group? The four squadrons of African-American airmen were now flying together as a well-trained and battle-tested group. The missions were just as dangerous as ever for both the fighter aircraft and the American bombers. Enemy fighters were always a concern, but as I said before, the biggest danger was the antiaircraft fire from the guns on the ground.

"The African-American pilots knew they were as good as the German and Italian fighter pilots who tried to attack the Allied bombers they had been assigned to protect. That was usually a one-on-one battle, but the enemy antiaircraft fire was another story. There was virtually nothing they could do about it. American bomber and fighter pilots dreaded the thick black smoke and debris from exploding shells, which was known as flak. The German 88-millimeter antiaircraft guns could fire about twenty shells per minute. A lot of the pilots joked that the enemy flak was so thick that they could walk on it."

Luis wanted to know something. "Mr. Kennedy, were a lot of bombers hit by enemy ground fire?"

"They sure were. Why? The answer is easy. The best protection in the air couldn't protect airplanes from the German guns on the ground. Two missions on July 19 and 20 are good examples of what it was like. On July 19, fifty-one P-51 Mustangs from the 332nd Fighter Group were given the job of protecting a group of American bombers that was assigned a bombing run to Munich, Germany.

"The bombers and their fighter escorts were located at different bases. At a predetermined spot, the two groups would meet, and then they'd continue on to the target area together. Everything was going well as the bombers dropped their bombs on the target. As they were leaving, they saw only four German fighters that were very far away. All was well, right? Wrong! The danger wasn't from the enemy airplanes. Although the German fighter planes had not attacked, German antiaircraft guns had hit two of the American B-24 bombers. One had only minor damage and was able to make its way to safety. Unfortunately, the other American B-24 took a major hit. As it exploded, men died.

"The next day, the African-American pilots were again assigned to provide protection for the bombers as they flew to Germany. All of a sudden, out of nowhere, twenty German fighters attacked the American airplanes as they got close to the target."

"Mr. Kennedy, how could the enemy airplanes make a surprise attack? Weren't the bomber and fighter pilots looking for them?"

"Of course they were, Marcus," said Kennedy. "They were constantly searching the skies for enemy airplanes. This particular time, the Germans attacked from the rear, hoping to catch the tail end of the bomber formation unprotected. Other times, they might fly several thousand feet higher than the formation and then dive at the bombers at a very high speed. In this case, when the Germans attacked, the Tuskegee Airmen quickly cut them off and shot down four of the enemy airplanes. While all of this was going on, the bombers kept flying toward their target.

"So once again the mission was a success, yes? Well, not quite. They had bombed the target. Four enemy airplanes had been destroyed. On the other hand, German guns on the ground shot down at least three of the American B-24 bombers. So, you see, war was very dangerous. The German antiaircraft fire from the guns on the ground was deadly."

"That must've been horrible, Mr. Kennedy. I mean, to see that happen to people and not be able to do anything about it."

"Yes, Charlene," agreed Kennedy, "it was horrible. This is what the men on both sides faced each day. Whether they were American, British, German, Italian, or Japanese, this was what war was about. It was terrible. Many people were wounded. Millions lost their lives.

"I've already told you that a couple of the African-American pilots shot down several German airplanes in one day. Well, a young lieutenant named Lee Archer earned quite a reputation on October 12, one of the 332nd Fighter Group's most successful days. About seventy American P-51 Mustangs from all four squadrons attacked German targets on the ground. They destroyed targets of every kind—airplanes, locomotives, rail cars, trucks, guns, and barges.

"Flying at an altitude between nine thousand and twelve thousand feet, the Mustangs headed in a north-northeast direction toward Budapest, Hungary. The sky was overcast with heavy gray clouds. As the flight of American fighter planes neared Lake Balaton in the western part of Hungary, they spotted an unidentified biplane near an enemy airfield. Thinking it was an enemy airplane, the pilots from the 99th Fighter Squadron investigated.

"Only minutes later, the P-51s of the 302nd Fighter Squadron broke from the formation. They had sighted an enemy airplane near a second German airfield. The 100th and 301st Fighter Squadrons continued on track toward the target. Suddenly, several P-51s with yellow tails flew toward the two fighter squadrons. The 100th Fighter Squadron headed in their direction to forestall an attack and let them know they were friendly.

"Now alone, the thirteen pilots of the 301st Fighter Squadron headed east toward the Danube River. After two hours of flying, they finally neared the target area. Below them, approximately fifty oil barges floated on the Danube River. Swooping in, the P-51s spent the next ten minutes making several passes at the barges. By the time they were finished, they had completely destroyed four of the oil barges. Another eleven had suffered major damage.

"After leaving the formation, the fourteen P-51s of the 99th Fighter Squadron headed for the Kaposvar airfield. Flying in from the east, the African-American pilots attacked the airfield and a large number of enemy airplanes parked on the ground. Each of the P-51s was armed with six machine guns, three in each wing. As the airplanes swooped in with guns firing, it was like a Fourth of July celebration. With no flak or small-arms fire to worry about, the pilots made repeated passes against the field. In just fifteen minutes, they attacked the field nine times. The results were impressive. The P-51s destroyed eighteen enemy airplanes on the ground. Another eight had been severely damaged.

"Near the east coast of Lake Balaton, the 100th Fighter Squadron went after a variety of targets on the ground. In fifteen minutes, they totally wrecked a train, damaging three locomotives, three passenger cars, and thirty boxcars. On a nearby highway, they shot up twenty-five trucks. At a camouflaged factory surrounded by three parking lots, they repeatedly strafed forty-five more trucks.

"The 302nd Fighter Squadron, led by Captain Wendell Pruitt, headed for the sole enemy airplane, a Heinkel He-111 twin-engine bomber. Pruitt peeled off to attack the German bomber. Lee Archer, one of the seventeen P-51 pilots of the 302nd Fighter Squadron, suddenly spotted a large number of German airplanes. As the Americans turned toward the Germans, the fight was about to begin. Soon, machine guns were blazing. Archer had plenty of experience under his belt. With forty-six combat missions to his credit, he was already battle tested.

"Archer pulled around behind one of the German airplanes and began firing at it. As the German airplane caught fire, its pilot parachuted to the ground. Lieutenant Archer spied four more enemy airplanes flying below him and went after them. Catching them by surprise, he pulled in behind one of the Germans and followed him. At a distance of about two football fields, Archer began firing at the German. Archer's aim was deadly, as he raked the side of the German airplane with machine-gun fire. Suddenly, the left wing of the enemy airplane broke off. The German airplane spun into an earthward dive that ended when it smashed into the ground.

"The lieutenant wasn't finished yet. He maneuvered around behind yet another enemy airplane and opened up on him with his machine guns blazing. As the German pilot tried to escape, Archer's .50-caliber bullets tore into the tail of the fleeing airplane with a deadly thud. As the German airplane hurtled through the air at several hundred miles per hour, it trailed a ribbon of black smoke. Seconds later, the airplane was in flames.

"In a dogfight that only lasted fifteen minutes, Lieutenant Lee Archer shot down three German airplanes. His friend, Wendell Pruitt, destroyed two more. In all, the 302nd Fighter Squadron pilots shot down nine enemy airplanes. Captain Wendell Pruitt flew his last mission eleven days later and returned home to the United States after flying a total of seventy combat missions.

"You know, while war was really serious business, there were some light-hearted moments. For example, even though it was against the rules, Pruitt was well known for buzzing the operations building after each successful mission.

"The 302nd also hit a German airfield that day. It was an open target, with at least twenty enemy airplanes sitting on the ground. Encountering no enemy groundfire, the pilots made several passes at the field. They destroyed eight German airplanes and damaged another eight.

"Unfortunately, Lieutenant Walter McCreary's P-51 had been hit by enemy groundfire. After eighty-nine combat missions, his luck had run out. He was able to parachute out of his burning airplane, but once he landed on the ground, the Germans captured him. Walter McCreary spent the rest of the war in a German prisoner-of-war camp."

"Mr. Kennedy, what was it like being a prisoner of war?" asked Tiffany.

"Well," said Kennedy, "it wasn't a very pleasant experience. Thousands of American fliers ended up in prisoner-of-war camps during World War II. Obviously, their experiences were all different, but the one thing that they all had in common was that being a prisoner of war was not a good thing.

"The one objective most of the fliers had after crashing or parachuting was to avoid being captured by the enemy. Many of the men were hurt when they parachuted to the ground, but they still had to try to evade capture. Each man had his .45-caliber pistol for protection, but he also carried an escape kit. It included items such as candy bars, maps, safety pins, needles, thread, and fishing hooks—the kinds of things that he could use to feed himself, if he could manage not to get caught.

"But, you know, that was a very hard thing to do. The downed fliers were in a strange country. Many were injured. Enemy soldiers and civilians were hunting for them. Some managed to make it back to safety or were rescued, but unfortunately, many men were captured and ended up in German prisoner-of-war camps. Before they were taken to a camp, they were often subjected to some pretty harsh treatment. Some were shot. Angry villagers often beat up the captive soldiers as they were marched to the railroad station for shipment to a camp. As the American fliers were spit upon and attacked with bricks and clubs, the German guards usually stood by and allowed it to happen.

"When the Americans finally arrived at one of the several large German prisoner-of-war camps, things usually didn't get much better. Guards interrogated the prisoners for information. There was frequent physical punishment; discipline was harsh. Some of the men were placed into solitary confinement. Others lived in large barracks that could house several hundred people.

"There weren't many comforts. Showers were extremely infrequent, maybe once a month. Lice, fleas, and ticks were a real problem since clothing didn't get washed often. Many of the men were very hungry. The food they were given to eat barely kept them alive, let alone healthy. Red Cross relief packages filled with goodies, such as candy, soap, and some canned food, were really welcome.

"Boredom was certainly a big problem for the men. There were few books; sometimes there was a deck of cards to wile away the hours. One of the Tuskegee Airmen, Alexander Jefferson, made a whole series of drawings about his capture. The men spent a great deal of time thinking about home and loved ones. They also spent lots of time trying to come up with ways to escape from the camps. Anyway, make no mistake about it, the German prisoner-of-war camps were not very nice places." A single hand went up.

"Yes, Makayla?" asked Kennedy.

"Were the black and white prisoners kept together?"

"They were, and generally, there were no problems. Each of these men had two goals—to stay alive and to escape. For the most part, there was no time for racism. There were more important things to worry about." Another hand went up.

"Mr. Kennedy, is it true that there were prisoner-of-war camps in America?"

"That's a good question, Pham, and the answer is yes. There were many prisoner-of-war camps that housed German and Italian prisoners in this country."

"Mr. Kennedy, were the German and Italian prisoners treated better than the American prisoners?"

"I hope so, Pham," said Kennedy. "I certainly hope so. I should also tell you something else. At many of the bases in America where German and Italian prisoners of war were held, the prisoners received better treatment than the African-Americans who were serving our country in the armed forces. The German and Italian prisoners of war had many more privileges than the black soldiers had. Imagine how it must have felt to be refused admission to the base theater because you were black, while the Nazi prisoners of war were allowed to attend the movie. The difference was that they were white, even if they were the enemy. Think about how unfair that must have seemed." A hand nervously went up in the back of the room.

"Yes?" asked Kennedy.

"Mr. Kennedy, what was it like for the men who were in Europe?"

"Well, obviously, the men were there to fight a war. They were kept pretty busy. When the weather was good, the pilots might fly four or five missions each day. Of course, that meant that the mechanics and crew chiefs stayed really busy making sure that the airplanes were always ready to fly. When the weather wasn't good, things still needed to be done, even if they couldn't fly. And there was always more training.

"The camps they lived in were pretty basic. In rainy weather, they often found themselves in nearly knee-deep mud. Most of the men lived in tents or at least structures that started out as tents and were quickly turned into living quarters. Creativity won out as the men used scraps of wood, empty oil drums, sheet metal—anything that could be recycled—to make the tents a little bit more comfortable."

"Mr. Kennedy, it sounds pretty hard. Didn't they have anything to do for fun?"

"Well, Makayla, recreation was very important. There were rest camps where the men had a chance to enjoy a little civilization from time to time. Officers' and enlisted men's clubs offered an opportunity to unwind. USO shows came to the base to provide a little live entertainment. The base theater showed the latest movies from home. One squadron formed a drama group and put on plays. Another organized a chorus. Church services obviously were important.

"There were all kinds of sports, both informal as well as organized. Baseball, basketball, and touch-football teams played against other squadrons throughout Europe. On one visit to the base, world heavyweight boxing champ Joe Louis acted as referee for a squadron boxing match. As difficult as it might've been, the men tried to make life as normal as possible during their time in Europe."

"Tell us about some more of the missions, Mr. Kennedy," requested one of the students.

"Well, class, for several months, the 332nd had been assigned to the Fifteenth Air Force. Each day, weather permitting, the 332nd pilots took off from their base at Ramitelli, located on Italy's east coast, joined the bombers, and escorted them to and from the targets. Since the Fifteenth Air Force had five wings containing eighty-four bombardment squadrons, there was rarely a day without a mission.

"On October 13, 1944, all four of the 332nd Fighter Group's squadrons were assigned close-escort duty for the 304th Bomb Wing, meaning they had to make sure that enemy fighters didn't get close to the American bombers. The target was an oil refinery in Blechhammer, Germany.

"The pilots climbed out of their cots early that morning. The mission was scheduled to take off just after nine o'clock. Since there might not be another chance to eat for several hours, a visit to the mess hall was important. After breakfast, it was time for the mission briefing. The pilots needed to know what to expect—where the antiaircraft artillery or enemy fighters might be found. Following the briefing, the airmen headed for the flight line, where the mechanics had been working on the P-51 Mustangs for hours. The armorers had already loaded the bombs and ammunition. After the pilots made a quick walk-around inspection of their airplanes with their crew chiefs, they were ready to take off.

"Sixty-nine P-51s sat on the ground ready for the day's mission. Shortly before nine o'clock, the pilots made last-minute checks and then cranked up the engines. Minutes later, the sleek red-tailed

Mustangs began taking off. One after another, the P-51s lifted off from the temporary runway at Ramitelli. Seven of the P-51s experienced mechanical problems and returned to base. Two additional Mustangs returned with them, serving as their escorts in case of enemy attack.

"After flying for nearly two hours, the remaining sixty P-51 Mustangs met up with the bombers. Flying at an altitude of almost twenty-four thousand feet, the P-51s were constantly on alert for enemy airplanes. At about 11:30 A.M., the bombers flew over their target and released their bombs on the oil refinery more than four miles below. Heavy black smoke rose into the sky; the bombs had hit their objective.

"Heading back to base, both bomber crews and fighter pilots remained alert for German aircraft, but none appeared. Released from protecting the bomber convoy, the 332nd Fighter Group's pilots went in search of targets on the ground.

"The 100th Fighter Squadron pilots were the first to find one. Three of the squadron's P-51s strafed six boxcars sitting at a railroad siding with machine-gun fire. Four 99th Fighter Squadron pilots caught up with a train that was moving east from Bratislava, a city in former Czechoslovakia. When they opened fire on the train, a pair of locomotives and one flatcar were badly damaged. The 302nd Fighter Squadron also set their sights on a freight train, attacking it with a vengeance. They destroyed one locomotive and damaged twelve boxcars and fourteen coal cars. When hit by machine-gun fire, a small house that sat next to the railroad tracks exploded in flames."

Charlene asked, "Were people in the house, Mr. Kennedy? Did they get hurt?"

"No, Charlene, the house was just being used to store ammunition; no one lived there. Nonetheless, many civilians were wounded or, even worse, killed during the war. That's what I keep trying to emphasize. Combat isn't glamorous or exciting—it's dangerous and destructive. But let me finish telling you about this particular mission before class ends.

"Eight P-51s of the 302nd Fighter Squadron headed for a small German airfield. In spite of some small-arms fire, the Mustangs made several passes at the field. When the smoke of the attack had cleared, seven enemy airplanes that were on the ground had been destroyed. Six more German airplanes were badly damaged."

Chapter Seven

Almost Over

"Was that the end of the war, Mr. Kennedy? Did the men get to go home then?"

"Unfortunately, Pham, the answer is no. By late fall of 1944, the idea of celebrating Thanksgiving and Christmas at home was only a dream for most of the men. There were still many tough months of war to come, as the Germans continued to resist the Allied push in Europe. To make things even worse, with the winter fast approaching, the men frequently awakened to weather that was not suitable for flying.

"Many of the pilots of the 332nd Fighter Group had flown more than one hundred combat missions since their arrival in Europe. They'd earned the right to go home. In November alone, fourteen pilots, all combat tested and highly experienced, completed their tour of duty and shipped back to the United States. They would really be missed. Over half of those men had shot down at least one enemy airplane. Fifteen fresh faces who were trained and ready to make their own contribution replaced the departing pilots."

Marcus waved his hand. "Mr. Kennedy, what did the men do when they couldn't fly?"

"Well, the November weather might make flying impossible, but training still kept up on a daily basis. When they weren't training, the men of the 332nd Fighter Group stayed busy doing other things. As we talked about earlier, recreation was always important. After months of practice, the 100th Fighter Squadron's choral group and a quartet from the 302nd Fighter Squadron got their big break. They gave their first performance on the radio for the Mediterranean Church of the Air. A squadron newspaper printed its first edition. Toward the end of November, the 100th Fighter Squadron's enlisted men's club opened for business. When the weather was really bad, the men stayed indoors and enjoyed games of checkers and cards. Ping-Pong was always a favorite."

"Mr. Kennedy, it must've been very lonely for them, being so far away from their families, especially during the holidays. I wouldn't want to be away from home then." Several students nodded their heads in agreement with Tiffany.

"You're certainly right. The holidays were very hard because the men really missed their families, but every effort was made to keep the spirits of the men strong. Christmas packages had already started to arrive from friends and families back home. No one was forgotten on Thanksgiving Day either. In spite of the difficult conditions, the cooks prepared a Thanksgiving dinner with turkey and all of the trimmings.

"As usual, the 332nd Fighter Group protected the Fifteenth Air Force's bomber squadrons on missions deep into Germany. The bombers had just one goal—to destroy German oil refineries and the factories making airplanes and tanks. The fighter pilots also strafed railroads, ships, and trucks. Between November 16 and 19, the 332nd flew several major missions.

"That reminds me of something. You recall how we talked about the support personnel at Tuskegee, don't you? Well, their jobs were maybe even more important overseas. Not to mention the fact that they were certainly working in far more difficult conditions than at home. Over the years, the support personnel, the men and women who keep the military operating efficiently at home and overseas, haven't received their share of the credit. I guess it's natural to give the recognition to the pilots. After all, their jobs are probably a lot more exciting and glamorous than those of most of the people on the ground. Think about it, when's the last time you watched a movie or a television show about a cook, a mechanic, or even someone mopping floors?" The class laughed.

"But, you know," continued Kennedy, "there certainly is a great deal of truth to the old saying that an army travels on its stomach. People quickly become unhappy when they're hungry. You know, it took anywhere from ten to fifteen people on the ground to keep one pilot in the air. The ground crews were essential to keeping the airplanes ready for the missions. So, just remember how important these support personnel were in winning the war. One of these days, when you don't get the part-time job that you want and have to take a less exciting one, keep in mind that all jobs are important. Whether keeping a military operation or our daily lives running smoothly, it takes everyone working together to make a project successful.

"Most people just don't think about it, but a good boss does. General Nathan Twining, the commanding general of the Fifteenth Air Force, certainly realized the importance of support personnel. In late November of 1944, he visited the base at Ramitelli, Italy. Do you know why? He wanted to tell the mechanics who were responsible for keeping the airplanes flying how much he appreciated their hard work.

"Because of the bad weather, operations had to be cut back during November. The group's pilots shot down only one enemy aircraft during the entire month. Nonetheless, tragedy struck the group often. Captain William Faulkner of Tennessee was killed during a mission over Austria in the early part of November. Several other men assigned to the 332nd Fighter Group would also be killed or reported missing in action in November.

"We know how dangerous it was to be a pilot. I've told you about the enemy fighters and the German antiaircraft guns. But it could also be very dangerous on the ground. On November 24, Sergeant Percy Gary died in a motor-vehicle accident. Accidents in the air also took their toll. I told you earlier about a mission back in July, during which Roger Romine shot down an enemy airplane. Well, now Romine's luck ran out. On takeoff on November 16, the airplanes of Romine and William Hill collided. Romine was killed and Hill suffered major burns. After missions in November, Roger Gaiter, Quitman Walker, and Maceo Harris became prisoners of war, while Elton Nightingale also ended up missing in action and was later declared dead.

"Class, do you remember when we talked about segregation and how horrible it was?" Thirty heads nodded in unison.

"Well, I stressed that because I think it's a very important concept for you to understand. And I'm not telling you about people dying or getting hurt just to make this story exciting. Do you know why we're talking about these things?" Makayla's hand went up.

"Because war's not a game. It's not fun, is it, Mr. Kennedy?"

"No, it's not," agreed Kennedy. "War is a horrible thing, even if it's sometimes necessary, and as you can easily see, it's a terrible waste of many lives. Your point was a good one. War isn't a game or a movie. It's not like a television show. In real life, when people are killed, they stay dead. They don't get up and go home afterward. Always remember that.

"I told you earlier that November was kind of a quiet month because of the poor weather. Only one man in the group was able to paint a swastika on his airplane. Does anyone know what I'm talking about?" There was no response.

"Well, when a fighter pilot shot down an enemy airplane, he would paint a symbol of the defeated enemy on his airplane. In the case of the war in Europe, an American pilot would paint one swastika on his airplane for each German airplane he shot down. Does anyone know what a swastika is?" One hand rose.

"Yes?" asked Kennedy.

"Well," said Luis, "it was a symbol that the Nazis in Germany put on their flags and stuff—kind of like an 'x' only sideways."

"Very good," said Kennedy, "very good. Actually, before the Nazis adopted it, artists had used the symbol in their work for centuries. And for those of you who don't know what it looks like, let me draw it on the board for you—even though I'm not much of an artist," laughed Kennedy.

"On November 16," he continued, "the 332nd Fighter Group was assigned one of their typical large missions. This time, it was to accompany bombers from the 304th Bomb Wing as they flew to Munich, Germany. At ten o'clock in the morning, more than sixty P-51s lifted off the steel-planked runway. After takeoff, the red-tailed Mustangs headed north toward the target. After flying for over two hours, they finally met the bombers for the rest of the trip to Munich. Suddenly, two Messerschmitt Me-109s flew in from several thousand feet above and attacked six P-51s that were flying at an altitude of twenty thousand feet. One of the American fighters was damaged in the attack.

"Near Udine, in the northeastern section of Italy, one of the B-24 bombers needed to return to base because of mechanical problems. Three P-51s stayed with the bomber for protection as it struggled homeward. At around 1:30 P.M., six Messerschmitt Me-109s dived at the bomber. First flying in a stretched-out line, one following the next, and then flying in a circle, the German airplanes went after the bomber."

"And then what happened, Mr. Kennedy? Did the bomber get away?" Several students in the front row looked worried.

"Captain Luke Weathers of the 302nd Fighter Squadron peeled off from the P-51s and managed to pull in behind one of the Germans. Flying slightly to the left and then to the right in a maneuver that looked like the letter *S*, Weathers got to within one hundred yards of the enemy plane. As Weathers fired short bursts of machine-gun fire at the airplane in front of him, his .50-caliber shells found their mark. The German Messerschmitt began smoking and headed for the ground with Weathers in hot pursuit. Flying down to an altitude of only one thousand feet, Weathers finally pulled back on the controls and headed skyward as the enemy airplane crashed into the ground.

"Looking around, Weathers spotted a Messerschmitt Me-109 behind him. The German pilot was obviously trying to shoot down Weathers' airplane. Both Weathers and the German flew through the air at several hundred miles per hour. Captain Weathers took a chance and cut back on his throttle, slowing his Mustang. As the German pilot maintained his speed, he flew past Weathers. With a clear advantage, Luke Weathers seized his opportunity. He fired at the enemy airplane that was now in front of him, causing the German pilot to crash into the side of a mountain. In only a few minutes, Captain Luke Weathers had shot down two enemy fighters. Meanwhile, the ailing American bomber made it safely back to its base."

"All right! Way to go, Captain Weathers!" The students looked much happier, until Kennedy continued with the story.

"A mission on November 19 didn't go as well. That day, two pilots from the 332nd Fighter Group became prisoners of war in German camps.

"Late that morning, the men climbed into their P-51s and headed for Austria and Hungary. The targets for the day would be railway, highway, and river traffic. After flying at about ten thousand feet for nearly two hours, the fifty P-51s split into two smaller groups. Airplanes from the 99th and 302nd Fighter Squadrons headed north, following the highway and railroad tracks toward Győr, Hungary. At the same time, the 100th and the 301st Fighter Squadrons flew to a destination slightly north of Lake Balaton in Hungary. Do you know where Austria and Hungary are?" asked Kennedy.

Most of the students nodded their heads, yes. Marcus raised his hand and said, "We studied that in geography last semester, Mr. Kennedy."

"Good," responded Kennedy as he continued the lesson. "Reaching their target area near Győr, fourteen pilots from the 302nd Fighter Squadron flew low and searched for targets to strafe on the ground. The 99th Fighter Squadron stayed high to provide protection from enemy aircraft. On the trip back to the base, the squadrons reversed positions, allowing the 99th to hit ground targets while the 302nd provided protection. Their attacks destroyed or damaged two locomotives, nearly a hundred railroad cars, and a large number of trucks.

"The results were much the same for the 301st and 100th Fighter Squadrons. Flying north of Lake Balaton and then to the south of Győr, the two squadrons strafed river traffic as well as trains and trucks along the highway. They destroyed one tank car and a dozen river barges and damaged a tugboat and several freight cars. Two 88-millimeter guns sitting on barges were also destroyed.

"The German antiaircraft guns had been busy. As the heavy flak hit the airplanes flown by Roger Gaiter and Quitman Walker, both pilots bailed out. Captured by the Germans, Gaiter and Walker would not be reunited with their fellow pilots of the 332nd Fighter Group until the end of the war."

"I'd hate to be away at war at Christmas time, Mr. Kennedy, but it'd be even worse to be a prisoner of war," commented Charlene.

"That would really be awful," agreed Tiffany.

"It would be, and it was," replied Kennedy. "The final month of 1944 brought much of the same weather as November had. Temperatures turned bitterly cold, with frequent rain. In spite of the weather and the holidays, the 332nd Fighter Group took part in twenty-two missions against German targets. On a mission on December 9, 1944, pilots of the 332nd Fighter Group were introduced to something they had been hearing about but hadn't seen firsthand. They came into contact with their first German jet fighter—the very fast, and obviously very dangerous, Messerschmitt Me-262."

"I didn't know there were jets back then, Mr. Kennedy."

"There were, Jamal, but they were brand new. In fact, aircraft companies in the United States were still working on them, but the Germans built them first. Let me tell you about that first encounter.

"All four squadrons of the 332nd Fighter Group provided escort cover for B-17s from the 5th Bomb Wing on a bombing run against Brux, Germany, on December 9, 1944. Known as a Flying Fortress, the four-engine B-17 was the largest airplane to see action during World War II. Over one hundred feet long, the big bomber made a very inviting target for German fighter pilots. The Tuskegee Airmen were determined to make sure that the bombers stayed safe from enemy fighter planes.

"Midmorning, fifty-four P-51s met the bombers over the northern part of the Adriatic Sea, just off the east coast of Italy. They spent the next hour and a half with the B-17s. Just before the P-51s left the bomber formation for their return to Ramitelli, they met up with the pride of the German aerial fleet—the Messerschmitt Me-262. Armed with four cannons, the twin-engine jet was capable of speeds over five hundred miles per hour. The Tuskegee Airmen were about to see it in action, up close and personal, for the first time.

"Far to the right of the large formation of American bombers, the African-American pilots observed five enemy aircraft. They were German jets and that meant trouble. For almost five minutes, the Germans flew parallel to the bombers. Then they flew away. Only five minutes later, another small formation of German jets was spotted.

"From an altitude of about thirty thousand feet, a single Me-262 traveled at a high rate of speed toward eight P-51 Mustangs. The German jet flew past the formation and went into a turn. Now, the German pilot was coming back. Attempting to cut him off, a P-51 pilot steered toward the German. The American fired his machine guns as the German pilot dived into the clouds below him. Within seconds, the German jet again headed for the formation of red-tailed Mustangs. Quickly covering a distance of ten thousand feet as he sped upward, the Me-262 disappeared into the gray cloud cover at thirty-five thousand feet.

"Minutes later, another American pilot encountered a German jet, perhaps the same one. The German pilot made a high-speed pass at the P-51. Closing to within a thousand yards, the American pilot began shooting at the jet, but it pulled away and was quickly out of range. That first meeting with the famous German jet was inconclusive, but there would be more to come."

"When, Mr. Kennedy? When would that happen?" Jamal demanded.

"Just be patient; I'll get to it. Don't worry." Kennedy continued. "As 1944 ended, the pilots of the 332nd Fighter Group flew their final mission of the year on December 29. The war against the Germans was winding down. Everyone predicted that victory was only a few months away, but it wouldn't come soon enough for many of the men. December had been a costly month. Andrew Marshall, Cornelieus Gould, and Lawrence Dickson all became prisoners of war. Frederick Funderburg, Earl Highbaugh, and James Ramsey died.

"During January 1945, bad weather greatly reduced flying operations. Rain, snow, and freezing weather caused many briefings to end with the announcement, 'No flying today.' A mission to Vienna, Austria, on January 21 led to the loss of two more pilots—both Albert Young and Samuel Foreman were shot down and listed as missing in action. February was another difficult month. Thomas Street, John Chavis, and Wendell Hockaday died in combat. Alfred Gorham and George Iles were listed as prisoners of war.

"As the war in Europe neared its end, the 332nd Fighter Group encountered few Germans in the air. Realizing that the Germans were barely able to offer opposition, American bombers continued to pound German industrial targets. Each day, if the weather allowed, formations of bombers and fighter airplanes ventured deep into German territory in an effort to completely subdue the enemy and end the war in Europe.

"Something very special happened in February. That month, the 332nd Fighter Group flew its two hundredth mission as part of the Fifteenth Air Force. During those two hundred missions, they had not allowed a single enemy fighter to shoot down an American bomber. Since they had transferred from the Twelfth Air Force to the Fifteenth Air Force, the 332nd Fighter Group had logged over eight thousand individual flights. The 332nd Fighter Group's pilots had received sixty-three Distinguished Flying Crosses for their service.

"During that same month, as the war continued to wind down, the 302nd Fighter Squadron had been deactivated. The 332nd Fighter Group was now made up of the 99th, 100th, and 301st Fighter Squadrons. Men who had proudly flown under the symbol of the 302nd Fighter Squadron, a red devil with wings, were either sent home—their overseas duty completed—or reassigned to the three remaining squadrons."

Chapter Eight

The Story Continues

"Mr. Kennedy, when did the war finally end?"

"Well, Luis," said Kennedy, "it's important to remember that the war was really being fought in two different areas at the same time. It was almost as if there were two separate wars. There was one being fought against the Japanese in the Pacific, and there was the one that we've been talking about in Europe, which was against the Italians and the Germans.

"Even as the war in Europe neared its end, several men in the 332nd would die. Others would spend the final months of the war in prisoner-of-war camps. By March, it was pretty obvious that the war in Europe was almost over, but there was still some rugged fighting ahead. A mission late that month earned the 332nd Fighter Group the Distinguished Unit Citation."

"What'd they do, Mr. Kennedy?" Pham asked. "What'd they do to get that? Did they shoot down more enemy airplanes?"

"They did that," said Kennedy, "and much more. Let me tell you about the mission that they flew on March 24. The night before, Colonel Davis informed the maintenance crews of the plans for the next day's mission. It was to be a long flight, nearly sixteen hundred miles round trip, but the P-51s couldn't fly that far without refueling. The only way that the P-51s could carry enough fuel to make the trip was to have the crews install extra-large external fuel tanks. The mechanics worked straight through the night. By sunup, they had equipped the P-51s with the larger tanks, allowing the flight to take place."

"Mr. Kennedy, that was another time that showed how important the support people really were, wasn't it?"

"It certainly was, Makayla. Without their efforts, the Tuskegee Airmen would never have been able to make a trip of that distance. The mission was a B-17 bombing raid against the Daimler-Benz Tank Assembly plant in Berlin, Germany. It was going to be a very long day. Nearly sixty P-51s rumbled down the runway at Ramitelli. By ten o'clock, they were all in the air and headed north-northeast. Minutes before noon, they met the bombers that were flying at an altitude of twenty-five thousand feet in the eastern part of Czechoslovakia. From there, they headed north. Berlin was about three hundred miles away.

"Less than fifty miles from the Berlin target area, thirty-five enemy airplanes were spotted, lying in wait. All that stood between the American bombers and the enemy were the Tuskegee Airmen. Things were about to become interesting.

"At an altitude of twenty-six thousand feet, four German jets attacked the last group of B-17 bombers. The Messerschmitt Me-262s were driven back; two of the jets were damaged. Then a single Me-262 headed for the red-tailed Mustangs. After one high-speed pass, the German jet flew away.

"At 12:15, three of the German jets flew in high, setting their sights on the lead group of bombers. The P-51s went after them, damaging one of the jets. Like a swarm of mosquitoes, the enemy airplanes kept buzzing around the bombers. Growing ever bolder as the American airplanes neared Berlin, ten enemy aircraft flew through the formation of bombers. For the next fifteen minutes, seventeen P-51 fighter pilots fought the Germans. With several bursts of machine-gun fire from his P-51, Roscoe Brown, of the 100th Fighter Squadron, became the first African-American airman to shoot down a German jet. Charles Brantley and Earl Lane, members of the same squadron, quickly brought down two more. When the smoke of battle cleared, three German jets had fallen to the Tuskegee Airmen.

"At the same time, a little to the west, seven more Me-262s encountered the P-51 pilots. The Germans divided into two smaller formations, with four planes in one group and three in another. Cannons blazed. One of the jets hit its target, scoring a direct hit on a P-51. The American pilot, Captain Armour McDaniel, parachuted from his burning airplane.

"The results of the day's mission were extraordinary. The mission had been one of the longest of the war. The number of enemy aircraft destroyed or damaged in the air was impressive. Three of Hitler's German jets had been shot down, and several others had been damaged. For its actions, the 332nd received a unit citation. But war always has its price. At least one of the B-17s had been hit by flak near Prague. There were probably no survivors. Captain Armour McDaniel, commanding officer of the 301st Fighter Squadron, had been shot down and would be held in a prisoner-of-war camp.

"Although the war in Europe was almost over, there were still missions to be flown and targets to be bombed. The War Department knew that unless the enemy was completely conquered, they would never accept a peace agreement. The pilots of the 332nd flew a very successful mission on April 1, shooting down twelve enemy airplanes. It was certainly a banner day for Harry Stewart, who downed three of them, but it was also a sad day. Walter Manning and William Armstrong both died during the mission.

"The 332nd flew its last combat mission on April 26. The Germans surrendered on May 8, 1945. The war in Europe was finally over."

"Mr. Kennedy, that must've been a great day," said Charlene.

"It was great beyond imagination, class. The war in Europe had been going on for so many years. It was just wonderful when it finally ended. The celebration was long overdue. The men who had been prisoners of war were freed and returned to base. Some of the men from the 332nd returned home in July. Most remained in Europe until October, since it took quite awhile to transport all of the American military personnel back to the United States."

"Mr. Kennedy, the Tuskegee Airmen did good, didn't they?"

"They sure did, Tiffany. The Tuskegee Airmen did a great job. But the sad thing was that when they returned to the United States, very little had changed. The country was still segregated. When they arrived in New York, there were many signs welcoming the troops home. But do you know what the African-Americans saw? As they got off the ship, they saw signs directing whites in one direction and African-Americans in another. We were still separated. We were still treated differently. We were still segregated after having done so much. It was very sad."

"Mr. Kennedy, how do you know so much about the Tuskegee Airmen? I mean, World War II was a really long time ago. But, then again, you're pretty old. Did you know some of them?"

"Well, Marcus, the way you said that might not be very flattering, but you're right on both counts. World War II was a long time ago and I am pretty old. And yes, I did know some of them. In fact, they were my friends, my buddies. You see, I am a Tuskegee Airman."

"Wow! You mean it? Aw' right! Way to go, man!" Exclamations rang out around the room. Pham raised his hand. "Mr. Kennedy, are you the only one left? Are there still other Tuskegee Airmen? Do they live around here? Do you know them?"

Kennedy laughed at all the questions. "No, I'm not the only one. There are still others, but some of us have died or are in ill health. Those of us who are left are all pretty old now, you know. Some of us are here in Washington, D.C.; others live in towns all over the country. And yes, I know them. Because of what we went through together, back then, we became really close friends. So we all stay in touch.

"There's something else that you also need to know. When a lot of people think of the Tuskegee Airmen, they think that the term refers just to the pilots. That's not right, though. Tuskegee Airmen aren't just pilots. All of the people who took part in the Tuskegee Experience—men and women, black and white, military and civilian, pilots and support personnel—are Tuskegee Airmen. Some of them might even be your neighbors. And while they don't brag about it, I'm sure they'd be happy to talk about their experiences if you ask. You see, everybody has his or her own story to tell."

Luis wanted to know, "How do we meet them, Mr. Kennedy?"

"Well, let me see what I can do," responded Mr. Kennedy. I'll talk to Mrs. Riggs and see if maybe we can arrange something. I'm sure some of the Tuskegee Airmen who live around here would come out to the school to talk to you all."

Heads nodded in agreement as Jamal spoke for all the rest of the students. "That'd be cool, Mr. Kennedy."

"But let me finish today's lesson, class. The story of the Tuskegee Airmen didn't stop with the end of the war. When the Tuskegee Airmen came back from Europe, life hadn't changed a lot in the United States for African-Americans. After all, this country was still . . ."

"Segregated?" asked Charlene. "No way, Mr. Kennedy. Didn't all the things that the Tuskegee Airmen accomplished make people see how wrong that was?"

"Unfortunately, class, it took a long time for that to change—a long time, a lot of people, and a lot more fighting—this time the fighting was not against an enemy overseas, but against discrimination right here in America. You've heard about the Civil Rights movement and everything that it achieved, I'm sure. But the accomplishments of the Tuskegee Airmen did play a part in that story. Let me explain.

"By the end of the war, nobody in the government or in civilian life could say that African-Americans weren't smart enough or brave enough to fly military airplanes. The men of the 99th Fighter Squadron, the 332nd Fighter Group, and the 477th Bombardment Group proved that wasn't true. What's more, their successes led to another major development.

"In 1948, President Harry S Truman issued Executive Order 9981, ending segregation in the U.S. military. That meant that all-black units like the 332nd and the 477th no longer officially existed. In the future, black and white Americans would serve side by side in the U.S. military. I'm not saying things changed overnight—it takes more than a presidential order to change the attitudes of people. Officially, though, segregation in the armed forces was a thing of the past. The Tuskegee Airmen helped to make that happen."

"It was about time," said several students.

"Past time," said Marcus.

"That's true," Kennedy replied. "But as I said, everything didn't change overnight. It took awhile. For example, let me tell you another story. The year before the president's order, the old Army Air Corps had become a separate branch of the military. Any guesses as to what it was called?"

"The Air Force, Mr. Kennedy?" answered Jamal.

"You've got that right," Kennedy responded. "And to its credit, the U.S. Air Force led the fight to integrate America's military in 1948. Everything wasn't great, though, even in the Air Force. In 1949, the Air Force held a fighter gunnery competition in Nevada. It was the first one of what would become a yearly event."

Tiffany waved her hand. "What's that mean, Mr. Kennedy? What's a fighter gunnery competition?"

"It was the first Top Gun contest. Airmen from units all over the country flew their airplanes in various contests to see who was the best at hitting targets, dropping practice bombs, things like that. At any rate, flying their old airplanes against the more modern aircraft that the other units had, the Tuskegee Airmen won the competition."

"All right! Yes!" came the cheers.

"Hold on. That's not the end of the story. The winners—the Tuskegee Airmen—were honored at a big banquet at a Las Vegas hotel. By the way, I should mention that this was the same hotel that, earlier in the week, had refused to serve several of the Tuskegee Airmen. Anyway, the trophies were awarded. Lots of pictures appeared in the newspapers. It was a really big deal. But a few years later, when the Air Force published a list of winners from each year, guess what happened? Somehow, the first winners were forgotten. The *Air Force Almanac* listed the winners of the first competition as 'unknown.' As I said, not everything had changed. It would take awhile."

"That's so wrong."

"It's just hateful."

"Bogus."

"All those things and more," agreed Kennedy. "A few years ago, several of the Tuskegee Airmen finally got the record corrected. After all, they knew who the winners had been. They'd been there. They'd received the trophies and had their pictures taken. They knew. Now, thanks to their efforts, everybody who reads the list knows. But we've always had to fight to get the credit that we deserved. Even today, most people don't know who the Tuskegee Airmen are or what we did."

"Maybe that's because World War II was such a long time ago," suggested Tiffany. "Maybe nobody remembers."

"Well, that might be part of the explanation. But it's still important to remember that the Tuskegee Airmen were part of the reason why today's military is made up of people of all races and backgrounds. You know from your history lessons that, unfortunately, there have been other wars since World War II. America has been involved in many of them. In fact, several of the Tuskegee Airmen fought for their country not just during World War II, but in several other wars as well."

Makayla announced proudly, "My sister's in the Air Force and she went to Bosnia during the war there a few years ago. Were some of the Tuskegee Airmen in Bosnia?"

"No, not in Bosnia. Most of the Tuskegee Airmen are my age or close to it. By then, we'd have been too old. However, after World War II, some of the Tuskegee Airmen fought in the Korean War. A few of us served in the Vietnam War in Southeast Asia during the 1960s and 1970s. For example, I belong to an organization called Tuskegee Airmen, Inc. One of the men who served several terms as president of our group, Charles McGee, flew more than four hundred combat missions during those three wars.

"But, Makayla, you mentioned that your sister served in the military during the war in Bosnia. Just think about what that means. Not only was her unit made up of people of all races and backgrounds, but now women also play much more active roles in the military. Jamal mentioned earlier that his father is in the army and that he's an African-American who commands white personnel. These kinds of things wouldn't have been possible before the Tuskegee Airmen proved to be so successful. There really have been a lot of changes since the days of World War II. We've made a lot of progress."

"Mr. Kennedy, tell us about some of the other Tuskegee Airmen. What happened to them?"

"Well, Luis, in the same way that all of you will go on to different jobs when you leave school, the Tuskegee Airmen went in different directions after the war. Some stayed in the military, where they had very successful careers and retired as high-ranking officers. For example, two of the best-known Tuskegee Airmen were Daniel 'Chappie' James, Jr., and Benjamin O. Davis, Jr. 'Chappie' James was a pilot in the 477th who stayed in the military and eventually became the very first African-American four-star general in the Air Force."

"What about Colonel Davis?" Charlene asked. "What happened to him?"

"He also stayed in the military, was promoted several more times, and eventually retired as a three-star general. In a ceremony held just a few years ago, the president of the United States, Bill Clinton, presented General Davis with his fourth star. It was a long-overdue recognition of his leadership.

"Those who left the service filled all kinds of jobs in civilian life, becoming everything from doctors, lawyers, and engineers to teachers, businessmen, and government officials. There are thousands of examples, but I'll tell you about just a few. Coleman Young served five terms as mayor of Detroit. William T. Coleman, Jr., became the national secretary of transportation in 1975. A gunner in the 477th Bombardment Group, Jean Esquerre left the military after the war to become an engineer. He was one of the first African-Americans to serve as a corporate director in the aerospace industry when he worked on the lunar module for the Apollo space program.

"Speaking of the space program, I'm sure you've seen launches of America's space shuttles on television. And, of course, you know that some of today's astronauts are African-Americans. You may not realize, however, that there were no black astronauts until Guion S. Bluford became the first African-American to fly in space in 1983. Four years later, Dr. Mae Jemison entered the history books as the first African-American woman to join NASA as an astronaut. While neither of them was a Tuskegee Airman, Guion Bluford had flown more than 140 missions in Southeast Asia as an Air Force pilot. Until the Tuskegee Airmen opened military aviation to African-Americans, his accomplishment wouldn't have been possible. In fact, many of the African-Americans involved in the space program today credit the Tuskegee Airmen with helping to pave their way to the stars." Pham raised his hand.

"Yes?" said Kennedy.

"Mr. Kennedy, this was a really good story. I mean, I really enjoyed it. But what does it have to do with the rest of us?"

"Do you mean those of you who aren't African-Americans?"

"Yeah, I guess that's what I'm asking. I mean, my family is from Thailand. And Luis is Hispanic. And Charlene's white. What's it have to do with us?"

"Well, the quick answer is that the story of the Tuskegee Airmen is not just a part of black history, but it's also an important part of American history. It's also a story that was untold for many years. There were no books, no movies, no television shows, and not even a mention in history classes. Because of that, most Americans, and that included a lot of African-Americans, didn't know what the Tuskegee Airmen did during World War II. They also didn't realize the long-term consequences of those accomplishments—results like the integration of our armed forces and, eventually, of American society in general.

"That's part of the story. The rest of my answer might sound a little corny, a bit old-fashioned, but I think it's perhaps the most important part. The Tuskegee Airmen showed the whole world what could happen when people have goals and keep trying, regardless of the obstacles put in their way, to achieve those objectives. The men and women who took part in the Tuskegee Experience had goals. The pilots wanted to fly military airplanes. The support personnel worked to help the pilots succeed. They all wanted to serve their country in a time of war. They never gave up, regardless of the difficulties or the opposition, and because of that, they were successful. Because of them and their determination, America is a better place, not just for African-Americans, but for everybody, regardless of race or sex or nationality.

"The job's not over yet. There's still a lot to be done, but the perseverance and hard work are just as important as they were back during World War II. And now, it's your turn."

Bibliography

Applegate, Katherine. *The Story of Two American Generals, Benjamin O. Davis, Jr., and Colin L. Powell.* New York: Dell Publishing, 1992.

Cooper, Charlie, and Ann Cooper. *Tuskegee's Heroes.* Osceola, WI: Motorbooks International, 1996.

Davis, Benjamin O., Jr. *Benjamin O. Davis, Jr., American.* Washington, D.C.: Smithsonian Institution Press, 1991.

Dryden, Charles. *A-Train: The Autobiography of a Tuskegee Airman Institution.* Birmingham, AL: University of Alabama Press, 1997.

Francis, Charles E. *The Tuskegee Airmen: The Men Who Changed A Nation.* Boston, MA: Branden Books, 1988.

Hardesty, Von, and Dominick Pisano. *Black Wings.* Washington, D.C.: Smithsonian Institution Press, 1984.

Harris, Jacqueline L. *The Tuskegee Airmen, Black Heroes of World War II.* Parsippany, NJ: Dillon Press, 1996.

Homan, Lynn M., and Thomas Reilly. *Black Knights: The Story of the Tuskegee Airmen.* Gretna, LA: Pelican Publishing Company, 2001.

Homan, Lynn M., and Thomas Reilly. *Images of America: The Tuskegee Airmen.* Charleston, SC: Arcadia Publishing, 1998.

Homan, Lynn M., and Thomas Reilly. *The Tuskegee Airmen Story.* Gretna, LA: Pelican Publishing Company, 2002.

Jakeman, Robert J. *The Divided Skies: Establishing Segregated Flight Training at Tuskegee, Alabama, 1934-1942*. Birmingham, AL: University of Alabama Press, 1992.

McGovern, James R. *Black Eagle: General Daniel "Chappie" James, Jr.* Birmingham, AL: University of Alabama Press, 1985.

McKissack, Patricia, and Fredrick McKissack. *Red-Tail Angels*. New York: Walker Publishing Company, 1995.

Rich, Doris. *Queen Bess, Daredevil Aviator.* Washington, D.C.: Smithsonian Institution Press, 1993.

Sadler, Stanley. *Segregated Skies: All-black Combat Squadrons of WWII.* Washington, D.C.: Smithsonian Institution Press, 1992.

Scott, Lawrence P., and William M. Womack, Sr. *Double V: The Civil Rights Struggle of the Tuskegee Airmen.* Ann Arbor, MI: Michigan State University Press, 1994.

Smith, Charlene McGee. *Tuskegee Airman: The Biography of Charles E. McGee.* Boston, MA: Branden Books, 1999.